Midwest Living® Magazine's

ALL-TIME
BEST
RECIPES

MIDWEST LIVING® MAGAZINE

Editor: Dan Kaercher

Managing Editor: Barbara Humeston

Food Editor: Diana McMillen

Art Director: Richard Michels

Test Kitchen Director: Sharon Stilwell

Contributing Food Editor: Barbara Albrecht

Publisher: Tom E. Benson

Project Development: Kathi Prien, Ellen de Lathouder

ALL-TIME BEST RECIPES

Project Editors: Spectrum Communication Services, Inc.

Graphic Designer: Michael Burns

Cover: Peachy Ozark Cobbler (see recipe, page 134)
Photograph: Mike Dieter. **Food Stylist:** Janet Pittman

Each recipe in this cookbook has been tested, evaluated and approved by the home economists in the Midwest Living® Test Kitchen.

ABOUT THIS COOKBOOK

From Ohio to Kansas, Michigan to North Dakota, you'll find America's best cooks right here in the Midwest. They're busy preparing delicious, satisfying dishes with the wonderful fresh ingredients that are so plentiful in America's Heartland.

As food editor of *Midwest Living*®, I've gotten to know dozens of delightful cooks during my travels around our region. I've also had the pleasure of sharing with our readers many cherished recipes from these talented individuals.

Over the years, many of our readers have written asking me to compile our recipes into a hardworking, "recipes-only" cookbook, much like the well-worn Midwest community and church cookbooks we all treasure. That's how ALL-TIME BEST RECIPES was born.

This book is a collection of my favorite recipes from the pages of our magazine. You'll find more than 200 in all, each one personally selected by me.

To make the book more useful, we've organized recipes into seven chapters, according to the type of recipe (Main Dishes, Breads, Desserts, etc.). Each recipe is presented in easy-to-follow, step-by-step fashion, along with a bit of information about who created the recipe or where it originated. Our special thanks to all the great Midwest cooks represented here!

At the end of the recipe chapters, on page 163, you'll find a chapter of menu ideas for special occasions and casual dining. We've also compiled two easy-to-use indexes, beginning on page 171, to help you locate any recipe in a jiffy: the first by recipe title and main ingredient, the second by state of origin.

I hope these recipes bring you as much pleasure as they've given me and my family and friends. Happy cooking—and eating!

—Diana McMillen
Food Editor, *Midwest Living*®

P.S. I'd like to hear your comments about ALL-TIME BEST RECIPES. Write to me at: MIDWEST LIVING®, 1912 Grand Ave., Des Moines, IA 50309-3379.

MAIN DISHES

Nut 'n' Cinnamon Pork

MAIN DISHES

BEEF
Cheeseburger and
   Fries, 21
Chilled Pepper Steak
   with El Tigre Sauce, 8
Cornish Pasties, 10
Country Steak Kabobs, 9
Dutch Spiced Beef, 9
Eight-Layer Casserole, 14
Glop, 16
Judie's Extra-Meaty Short
   Ribs, 12
Luxembourg Meat-and-
   Cabbage-Filled
   Packets, 20
Mike's Ribs and
   Kraut, 11
Norwegian Meatballs, 19
Pepper-Herb Rib
   Roast, 7
Puffed-Up Pizza
   Casserole, 15
Quick-and-Easy
   Pasties, 11
Ranch-Style Brisket, 13
Sacred Heart
   Meatballs, 18
Sacred Heart Meat
   Sauce, 17

CHICKEN
Bow-Tie Chicken
   Salad, 31
Chicken with
   Horseradish Cream, 28
Chick's
   Divan, 30
Cranberry Chicken, 29
South-of-the-Border
   Grilled Chicken
   Salad, 27
Unforgettable Chicken
   Pie, 32

EGGS AND CHEESE
Egg-Potato Scramble, 38
Monterey Jack Cheese
   and Egg Casserole, 38

FISH
Buttermilk-Pecan
   Catfish, 37

HAM
Beer-Glazed Ham, 25
Hash Brown-Ham
   Casserole, 26
Swedish Christmas
   Ham, 25

PORK
Apricot-Glazed Canadian
   Bacon, 26
Arrorsto Vitello Maile
   (Veal and Pork
   Roast), 22
Cherries and Chops, 23
Italian Porketta, 23
Nut 'n' Cinnamon
   Pork, 24

SEAFOOD
Cyndi's Seafood
   Lasagna, 36

STUFFINGS
Apple-Apricot
   Stuffing, 35
Chestnut Dressing, 35
Loggers' Vegetable
   Stuffing, 34

TURKEY
Gridiron Grilled Turkey
   with Tomato
   Chutney, 33
Turkey Tenderloin with
   Green Onions, 34

VEAL
Kalber Baelleli (Swiss
   Veal Balls), 21

PEPPER-HERB RIB ROAST

Beef roast often highlights the holiday bill of fare at the Des Moines Living History Farms'
1900s farmhouse. Here's an updated, fancy herbed version using a standing rib roast.

4   teaspoons cracked black
    pepper
1   teaspoon garlic salt
½   teaspoon dried thyme,
    crushed
½   teaspoon dried
    marjoram, crushed
¼   teaspoon ground cloves
¼   teaspoon fennel seed,
    crushed
1   5- to 6-pound standing
    beef rib roast
2   tablespoons lemon juice
    Grape leaves (available
    from a florist)
    Canned crab apples
    Kumquat Flowers

1. Combine pepper, garlic salt, thyme, marjoram, cloves and fennel.

2. Brush the roast with lemon juice. Rub pepper mixture over roast.

3. Place meat, fat side up, in a 15½x10½x2-inch roasting pan. Insert meat thermometer.

4. Roast in a 325° oven for 2 to 3 hours for rare (140°), 2½ to 3¾ hours for medium (160°) or 3 to 4¼ hours for well-done (170°).

5. Cover with foil and let stand for 15 minutes before carving. Garnish the platter with grape leaves, crab apples and Kumquat Flowers. Makes 15 to 18 servings.

KUMQUAT FLOWERS: Using *fresh kumquats*, score just through the peel up from the base, over the top and down to the base again. Score the fruit into fourths or sixths. Pull peel back for the "petals" of flower.

Note: The roast will continue to cook some while standing. If you like, remove the roast when the thermometer registers 5° below the desired doneness.

CHILLED PEPPER STEAK WITH EL TIGRE SAUCE

You can serve this as a luncheon entrée, but at The Buxton Inn in Granville, Ohio, it's a popular appetizer. A piquant horseradish sauce tops the tender chilled beef slices.

4 or 5 slices whole wheat, rye and/or pumpernickel bread (½ inch thick), quartered

¼ cup butter or margarine, melted

2 tablespoons cracked black peppercorns

¼ cup clarified butter or margarine (see directions at the end of Buttermilk-Pecan Catfish recipe, page 37)

2 10-ounce lean beef strip steaks (cut ¾ to 1 inch thick), trimmed of fat

El Tigre Sauce

Flowering kale or lettuce leaves

Lemon wedges, tomato wedges and sweet pickles

1. For croutons, place bread pieces in large bowl. Drizzle with ¼ cup melted butter or margarine. Toss to coat. Arrange coated bread pieces in a single layer on baking sheet. Bake in 300° oven for 10 minutes. Turn pieces. Bake for 5 minutes more or till bread is dry and crisp. Remove from oven. Set aside.

2. Press peppercorns into the steak.

3. In a large, heavy skillet, heat clarified butter or margarine. Add steaks. Cook over medium-high heat for 7 to 9 minutes or till steaks are of desired doneness, turning occasionally.

4. Remove steaks from skillet. Cool and chill.

5. Prepare the El Tigre Sauce.

6. To serve, line 4 or 5 individual plates with flowering kale or lettuce leaves. On each plate, place 4 croutons on leaves. Slice steaks thinly. Arrange a slice of steak on each crouton. Spoon about 2 tablespoons of the El Tigre Sauce over each serving. Garnish with a lemon wedge, tomato wedge and pickle. Makes 4 or 5 servings.

EL TIGRE SAUCE: In a bowl, combine ½ cup *mayonnaise* or *salad dressing*, 1 to 2 tablespoons *prepared horseradish*, 2 teaspoons snipped *parsley* and ½ teaspoon *lemon juice*. Cover the mixture and chill.

DUTCH SPICED BEEF

A spicy rubdown gives pot roast an Old World touch. This is the way it's served in Dutch communities from Michigan to Iowa.

1 3- to 4-pound boneless beef chuck pot roast, about 2 inches thick
2 teaspoons ground allspice
2 teaspoons salt
¼ teaspoon pepper
¾ cup beef broth or water

1. Trim excess fat from meat; reserve trimmings. Cut meat in half lengthwise and horizontally, almost through, forming two 1-inch connected portions. Lay flat. Mix allspice, salt and pepper. Rub inside of meat with about half the spice mixture. Roll up meat; tie with string. Rub outside with remaining mixture.

2. In a Dutch oven, heat trimmings till 2 tablespoons of hot fat accumulate; discard trimmings. (If meat is lean, add cooking oil to make 2 tablespoons.) Brown meat in hot fat. Add broth. Cover; simmer 1¾ to 2¼ hours or till tender. Remove from pot. For gravy, thicken cooking liquid. Makes 8 servings.

COUNTRY STEAK KABOBS

The whole county turns out when Kevin Irsik of Ingalls, Kansas, barbecues these flavorful kabobs or any of his other beef and sausage specialties.

1 pound beef sirloin or top round steak
1 5½-ounce can tomato juice (⅔ cup)
¼ cup ketchup
¼ cup white vinegar
2 to 3 tablespoons prepared mustard
1 tablespoon packed brown sugar
8 mushrooms
8 chunks fresh pineapple
1 green pepper
4 cherry tomatoes

1. Cut beef into 1½-inch pieces. Place beef in a bowl. Mix together tomato juice, ketchup, vinegar, mustard, brown sugar, ½ teaspoon *salt* and ½ teaspoon *pepper*. Pour over beef. Cover; chill for 1 to 2 hours.

2. Drain beef, reserving sauce. Cut green pepper into 8 squares. On 4 long skewers, alternate beef cubes with mushrooms, pineapple chunks and green pepper.

3. Grill over *medium-hot* coals, basting frequently with sauce, to desired doneness, about 15 minutes for rare. Garnish end of each skewer with a cherry tomato. Serves 4.

CORNISH PASTIES

Mona Abel, supervisor at Ironworld USA near Chisholm, Minnesota, gets together with her family to make dinner-plate-size pasties (PASS-tees). Here's a smaller version of Mona's Cornish recipe for those tasty piecrust pockets, packed with meat and potatoes. Residents of Iron Country in northern Minnesota top their pasties with butter or ketchup. You can try gravy, sour cream or plain yogurt, too.

4	cups all-purpose flour
1	teaspoon salt
1	cup lard or shortening
¾ to 1	cup water
3	cups finely chopped, peeled potato
1	pound beef round steak, cut into ¼-inch cubes
1½	cups finely chopped onion
1½	cups finely chopped, peeled rutabaga
8	teaspoons butter or margarine

1. For pastry, in a mixing bowl, combine flour and salt. Cut in lard or shortening till mixture forms pieces the size of small peas.

2. Stir in water, a tablespoon at a time, till mixture forms a ball. Divide dough into 8 equal portions.

3. On a lightly floured surface, roll out each ball to form an 8-inch circle, trimming off uneven edges.

4. In another bowl, toss together potato, steak, onion and rutabaga. Place 1 cup (one-eighth) of the mixture on one side of each circle. Top each with 1 teaspoon of the butter or margarine and sprinkle with some salt and pepper.

5. Moisten edges of dough with water and fold over to form a half-moon shape. Crimp edges with a fork.

6. Place on 2 shallow ungreased baking pans or 2 baking sheets. Bake in a 375° oven for 40 minutes. Makes 8 servings.

Note: Save time by chopping the vegetables in your food processor.

QUICK-AND-EASY PASTIES

These pasties are a shortcut version of the ones residents of northern Minnesota's Iron Country enjoy. They're perfect when time is scarce and leftovers plentiful.

½ package 9-inch folded refrigerated unbaked piecrust (1 crust) or 1 tube refrigerated pastry pockets

⅔ cup ¼-inch cubes cooked beef, pork or lamb

⅔ cup any combination of diced, cooked vegetables, such as potato, carrot, turnip, rutabaga or corn or peas

3 tablespoons chopped onion

1 tablespoon steak sauce Ketchup

1. Prepare piecrust according to package directions. Meanwhile, in a bowl, combine meat, vegetables and steak sauce; toss lightly.

2. Cut piecrust into 4 equal pieces along creases, or prepare pockets according to package directions. Spoon about ⅓ cup of the meat mixture onto half of each piece of piecrust or pocket. Moisten piecrust edges. Fold other half of piecrust or pocket over meat. Seal edges by crimping with a fork. Place pasties on ungreased baking sheet.

3. Bake in a 375° oven, piecrust pasties for 30 minutes or till crust is browned, pocket pasties for 12 to 17 minutes or till golden. Serve hot or cold with ketchup. Makes 4 servings.

MIKE'S RIBS AND KRAUT

Mike Fuss, a fireman and firehouse cook in Madison, Wisconsin, says this hearty one-dish meal is popular with new and veteran firefighters alike.

4 pounds beef back ribs (mix in short ribs, if desired), 6 to 8 ribs

4 Idaho or Russet potatoes, unpeeled and cut up

1 bunch carrots, unpeeled and cut into 2-inch pieces

4 medium onions, halved

1 27-ounce can sauerkraut

1. In a 6-quart Dutch oven, arrange half the beef back ribs on the bottom of the pot. Cover the ribs with layers of the unpeeled, cut-up potatoes, carrot pieces and halved onions. Top that mixture with the remaining ribs.

2. Spoon *undrained* sauerkraut over meat and vegetable mixture in Dutch oven. Cover and bake in 300° oven for about 4 hours or till meat is done.

3. Drain the juice from the meat mixture and save it to use later for soup or gravy. Season the meat and vegetables with *pepper*. Serves 6.

JUDIE'S EXTRA-MEATY SHORT RIBS

Judie Weil of St. Louis Park, Minnesota, buys "St. Louis ribs" with the top layer of meat and fat already removed. She's discovered that these ribs from the chuck are meatier than short ribs from the rib section and cook faster.

6 to 8 pounds beef-chuck short ribs
½ cup soy sauce
¼ cup cooking oil
1 teaspoon brown sugar
1 teaspoon cracked black pepper
6 green onions, thinly sliced

1. If necessary, remove top layer of meat and fat from ribs. Trim fat from meat. Score meat every ½ inch.

2. In a large, shallow container, stir together soy sauce, cooking oil, brown sugar, cracked black pepper and thinly sliced green onions. Add short ribs, turning to coat. Cover; refrigerate 3 to 24 hours.

3. Drain ribs, reserving marinade. Barbecue ribs on a covered grill directly over *medium-hot* coals for about 30 minutes, turning occasionally and brushing with reserved marinade. (Or, in a covered grill, arrange *medium-hot* coals around a drip pan. Test for *medium* heat above drip pan. Place meat, bones side down, on grill rack over drip pan. Grill, covered, for about 45 minutes or till ribs are the desired doneness.) Makes 6 to 8 servings.

Note: Be sure to use the beef-chuck short ribs as specified. Any other cut of ribs needs to be cooked longer.

Nutrition Note: To lower the sodium content of this dish, use sodium-reduced soy sauce.

RANCH-STYLE BRISKET

Texas-born Gloria Sextro nows lives in St. Louis, Missouri, but still brings the unique influence of the Lone Star State to her barbecue. Her burgundy marinade adds a rich and spicy flavor to the beef.

1   4-pound fresh beef brisket
5   cloves garlic
1   teaspoon crushed black peppercorns
2   cups burgundy
½   cup bottled barbecue sauce
½   cup chopped onion
3   tablespoons soy sauce
2   tablespoons red wine vinegar
2   tablespoons Worcestershire sauce
2   teaspoons liquid smoke
1   teaspoon celery seed
½   teaspoon garlic salt
2   cups bottled barbecue sauce
½   cup chopped onion
¼   cup burgundy
1½ teaspoons Worcestershire sauce
1½ teaspoons pepper
½   teaspoon salt

1. Rub the fresh beef brisket with the garlic and crushed peppercorns.

2. In a plastic bag set in a large bowl, combine the 2 cups burgundy, ½ cup barbecue sauce, ½ cup onion, soy sauce, vinegar, 2 tablespoons Worcestershire sauce, liquid smoke, celery seed and garlic salt.

3. Place the meat, fat side down, in bag. Seal bag and marinate in the refrigerator for 6 hours or overnight. Remove meat from bag and discard marinade.

4. For sauce, combine the 2 cups barbecue sauce, ½ cup onion, ¼ cup burgundy, 1½ teaspoons Worcestershire sauce, 1½ teaspoons pepper and salt.

5. Place the meat on 2 large sheets of heavy-duty foil (each about 30x18 inches). Pour sauce over meat. Seal the foil around the meat.

6. Cook meat in a smoker, according to manufacturer's directions, for 6 to 8 hours or till done. (Or, bake in a 325° oven for 3 hours or till very tender.)

7. To serve, trim off any blackened crust and the fat. Slice or chop for sandwiches and serve with your favorite barbecue sauce. Makes 12 to 16 servings.

Note: The Sextros use KC Masterpiece Barbecue Sauce for this recipe.

EIGHT-LAYER CASSEROLE

From Waukegan, Illinois, Michelle Crombie's hotdish has been to almost as many church suppers as she has. It boasts a hearty tomato sauce, a smooth cream-cheese filling, chopped spinach and cheddar cheese.

1   pound ground beef
2   8-ounce cans tomato
    sauce
1   teaspoon dried basil,
    crushed
½   teaspoon sugar
½   teaspoon garlic powder
¼   teaspoon salt
¼   teaspoon pepper
1   cup dairy sour cream
1   8-ounce package cream
    cheese, softened
½   cup milk
2   tablespoons chopped
    onion
6   ounces noodles, cooked
    and drained
1   10-ounce package frozen
    chopped spinach,
    cooked and well-
    drained
1   cup shredded cheddar
    cheese (4 ounces)

1. In a large skillet, cook beef till brown. Drain off fat.

2. Stir in tomato sauce, basil, sugar, garlic powder, salt and pepper. Bring to boiling. Reduce heat and simmer beef mixture, uncovered, for 5 minutes.

3. Combine sour cream, cream cheese, milk and onion. In a greased 2-quart round casserole or a 2-quart square baking dish, layer *half* the noodles, *half* the meat, *half* the cream-cheese mixture and all the spinach. Top with the remaining meat and noodles.

4. Cover; bake in 350° oven for 45 minutes. (Chill remaining cream-cheese mixture.) Spread with cream-cheese mixture. Top with the cheddar cheese.

5. Bake, uncovered, for 10 minutes more. Makes 6 servings.

PUFFED-UP PIZZA CASSEROLE

This Italian-style hotdish tastes great and freezes well, which makes it perfect for the hectic lifestyle of Sue and Loren Erickson of Maryland Heights, Missouri.

1½ pounds ground beef
1 15-ounce can tomato sauce
1 cup chopped onion
1 cup chopped green pepper
½ cup water
1 1½-ounce package spaghetti sauce mix
1 teaspoon dried oregano, crushed
1 clove garlic, minced
 Several dashes bottled hot pepper sauce
1 cup milk
¼ cup butter or margarine, melted
1 tablespoon cooking oil
2 eggs
1 cup all-purpose flour
8 ounces shredded mozzarella cheese (2 cups)
½ cup grated Parmesan cheese (2 ounces)

1. In a 12-inch skillet, cook the ground beef till brown. From the meat, drain off the fat and discard it.

2. Stir in the tomato sauce, chopped onion, chopped green pepper, water, spaghetti sauce mix, oregano, minced garlic and bottled hot pepper sauce. Bring to boiling. Reduce heat and simmer mixture, covered, for 10 minutes.

3. Meanwhile, in a small mixer bowl, beat the milk, melted butter or margarine, oil and eggs for 1 minute with an electric mixer on medium speed. Add flour; beat for 2 minutes more.

4. Turn meat mixture into a 13x9x2-inch baking pan; sprinkle with mozzarella. Top with flour mixture. Sprinkle with Parmesan. Bake in a 400° oven for about 30 minutes or till puffed and golden.

5. Let the hotdish stand for 10 minutes before eating. Makes 10 servings.

GLOP

Talie Meyer McKenzie of Arlington Heights, Illinois, says every cook who makes this dish must contribute a new ingredient. We added spaghetti sauce and the microwave version.

2	pounds ground beef
2	large onions, thinly sliced (3 cups)
1	cup chopped green pepper
1	28-ounce can tomatoes, cut up
1	15-ounce jar spaghetti sauce or pizza sauce
2	4-ounce jars sliced mushrooms, drained
½	teaspoon dried marjoram, crushed
¼	teaspoon dried oregano, crushed
¼	teaspoon pepper
2½	cups macaroni, cooked and drained
8	ounces cheddar cheese, cut into cubes
12	ounces Swiss cheese or mozzarella cheese, cut into cubes

1. In an 8-quart Dutch oven, cook the beef, onions and green pepper till the meat is brown and the vegetables are tender. Drain off fat from mixture.

2. Stir in the tomatoes, spaghetti or pizza sauce, mushrooms, marjoram, oregano and pepper. Heat the mixture to boiling. Reduce heat and simmer, uncovered, for 30 minutes.

3. Stir in the cooked macaroni and cheeses. Cook and stir till the cheeses melt. Makes 8 to 10 servings.

To Use Your Microwave
Cut recipe ingredients in half. In a 3-quart round casserole, microcook the beef, onion and green pepper on 100% power (high) for 6 to 8 minutes or till meat is brown and vegetables are tender; stir once. Drain off fat.

Stir in tomatoes, spaghetti sauce, mushrooms, marjoram, oregano and pepper. Microcook on high for 10 to 12 minutes more; stir once. Microcook on 50% power (medium) for 10 minutes, stirring occasionally.

Stir in the cooked macaroni and the cheeses. Microcook on high for 3 to 5 minutes or till the cheese melts. Makcs 4 or 5 servings.

SACRED HEART MEAT SAUCE

For their suppers, parishioners at Sacred Heart Church in Cincinnati, Ohio, cook meatballs in a locally produced and distributed sauce called Chef Tony's, which a church member, who's now deceased, created. The following recipe, provided by members of Sacred Heart, can be served by itself over spaghetti or with meatballs. The Sacred Heart cooks use Chef Tony's Sauce as an ingredient; for a substitute, they suggest Paul Newman's meatless spaghetti sauce (the national brand they consider most similar). "Fix the sauce at least one hour before serving so flavors will blend," the cooks say.

2 tablespoons chopped onion
1 tablespoon cooking oil, butter or lard
1½ cups sliced fresh mushrooms (optional)
12 ounces lean ground beef chuck
½ pound lean ground pork
1 tablespoon snipped parsley
1½ teaspoons salt
¼ teaspoon pepper
2¾ cups warm water
1 15-ounce can tomato puree
1 48-ounce jar meatless spaghetti sauce
1 bay leaf (optional)

1. In a Dutch oven or kettle, cook onion in oil till tender, but not brown. Add mushrooms, if you like; cook for 1 or 2 minutes.

2. Add ground beef and ground pork; brown. Drain off fat. Stir in snipped parsley, salt, pepper and *1¼ cups* of the warm water; simmer for 3 to 5 minutes.

3. Add tomato puree. Rinse can with *¼ cup* of the warm water; add to mixture. Simmer for 3 to 5 minutes.

4. Add meatless spaghetti sauce. Rinse jar with remaining *1¼ cups* warm water; add to mixture. Add bay leaf, if you like. Bring to boiling; reduce heat and simmer, uncovered, for 10 to 15 minutes. Makes about 10 cups sauce.

Note: You can freeze any leftover sauce .

SACRED HEART MEATBALLS

These meatballs disappear fast at suppers at Cincinnati's Sacred Heart Church and Italian Center.

4 or 5 ¾-inch slices Italian bread
2 eggs
½ cup fine, dry Italian bread crumbs
½ cup finely chopped Bermuda onion
½ cup grated Romano or Parmesan cheese or a blend of both
2 tablespoons snipped parsley
½ teaspoon salt
¼ teaspoon garlic salt
¼ teaspoon pepper
1 pound lean ground beef
½ pound lean ground pork
2 teaspoons olive oil or cooking oil
1 tablespoon cooking oil, lard or shortening
8 cups spaghetti sauce (use recipe on page 17 or use purchased spaghetti sauce)

1. Soak the bread slices in ½ cup *water* for a few minutes. Finely chop bread (you should have about 1¼ cups).

2. Beat eggs; stir in chopped bread, bread crumbs, onion, cheese, parsley, salt, garlic salt, pepper and 3 tablespoons *water*. Add meat to egg mixture; mix well. Work in olive oil or cooking oil.

3. Scoop out meat with No. 24 ice cream scoop (3 tablespoons per meatball). Wet hands; shape balls.

4. In a 12-inch skillet, slowly brown half of the meatballs in hot cooking oil, lard or shortening; remove from pan. Brown remaining meatballs. Drain off fat. (Or, transfer meatballs to a 13x9x2-inch baking pan. Omit cooking oil. Bake meatballs in a 350° oven for 20 minutes. Drain.)

5. Add meatballs to spaghetti sauce. Simmer, covered, for about 1 hour, stirring occasionally. Makes 24 meatballs.

NORWEGIAN MEATBALLS

A hint of spices flavors these tiny meatballs cooked in big batches for church suppers at Our Savior's Lutheran Church in rural Beldenville, Wisconsin.

1   beaten egg
⅓   cup milk
¼   cup fine, dry bread
      crumbs
1   tablespoon finely
      chopped onion
½   teaspoon salt
⅛   teaspoon ground allspice
⅛   teaspoon ground nutmeg
⅛   teaspoon pepper
¾   pound ground beef,
      triple ground
¾   pound ground pork,
      triple ground
3   tablespoons butter
¼   teaspoon salt
⅛   teaspoon pepper
½   cup milk
1   tablespoon all-purpose
      flour
½   cup milk

1. In a large bowl, combine egg, the ⅓ cup milk, bread crumbs, onion, the ½ teaspoon salt, allspice, nutmeg and ⅛ teaspoon pepper. Add beef and pork; mix well. Shape the meat mixture into 1-inch balls.

2. In a heavy 12-inch skillet, heat butter over medium heat. Cook meatballs slowly on all sides till well browned, shaking skillet frequently to help meatballs keep their shapes. With slotted spoon, remove meatballs from skillet; keep warm.

3. Drain fat from skillet. In a screw-top jar, combine the ½ cup milk, flour, the ¼ teaspoon salt and ⅛ teaspoon pepper; cover and shake till well combined. Stir into drippings in skillet. Stir in remaining ½ cup milk. Cook and stir over medium heat till thickened and bubbly. Cook and stir for 2 minutes more. If necessary, thin with a little more milk.

4. Transfer meatballs to gravy; heat through. Makes 42 meatballs; 6 main-dish servings.

Note: To assure the meatballs are the typical texture, ask your butcher to triple grind the meat. Ground beef and pork usually are ground just once.

LUXEMBOURG MEAT-AND-CABBAGE-FILLED PACKETS

Baking these savory buns helps Judy Nemmers rekindle the spirit of the Old Country in the tiny village of St. Donatus, Iowa.

1   **pound lean ground beef**
4   **cups shredded cabbage**
1   **small onion,**
      chopped (⅓ cup)
¼ **cup water**
1   **teaspoon salt**
½ **teaspoon caraway seed**
¼ **teaspoon garlic powder**
⅛ **teaspoon pepper**
     Yeast Roll Dough

1. In a skillet, brown beef; drain.

2. Stir in cabbage, onion, water, salt, caraway seed, garlic powder and pepper. Bring to boiling. Reduce heat. Cover; simmer 15 minutes.

3. Prepare the Yeast Roll Dough. Cover and let rest for 10 minutes.

4. Roll out Yeast Roll Dough to form a 20x15-inch rectangle. Cut into 3-inch circles of dough. Spoon about 2 tablespoons beef mixture onto center of each circle. Bring sides to center and pinch dough to seal.

5. Place bundles, seam side down, on greased baking sheet. Let rise in warm place for 45 minutes or till double.

6. Bake in a 375° oven for about 18 minutes or till golden. Makes 36.

YEAST ROLL DOUGH: Dissolve 2 packages active dry *yeast* in ¾ cup *warm water*. Add 2½ cups *all-purpose flour*, 1¼ cups *buttermilk*, ¼ cup *shortening*, 2 tablespoons *sugar*, 2 teaspoons *baking powder* and 1 teaspoon *salt*. Beat with an electric mixer for 30 seconds, scraping sides of bowl. Beat on medium 2 minutes, scraping occasionally. Using 2¼ to 2¾ cups *all-purpose flour*, stir in as much flour as you can. Turn out onto a floured surface; knead in enough remaining flour to make a moderately stiff dough that's smooth and elastic (6 to 8 minutes). Shape into a ball.

CHEESEBURGER AND FRIES

Rosemary Thomas of Elkader, Iowa, loves this quick-to-fix, stick-to-your-ribs casserole, which kids—of all ages—probably will want to douse with ketchup.

2   pounds lean ground beef
1   10¾-ounce can
     condensed golden
     mushroom soup
1   10¾-ounce can
     condensed cheddar-
     cheese soup
1   20-ounce package frozen,
     fried crinkle-cut
     potatoes
     Hamburger toppings
     (choose from ketchup,
     pickles, mustard and
     chopped tomato)

1. In a large skillet, cook the ground beef, half at a time, till brown. Drain off fat. Place the cooked meat in the bottom of a 3-quart rectangular baking dish.

2. In a medium mixing bowl, combine the condensed golden mushroom soup and the condensed cheddar-cheese soup. Spread over the meat in the casserole.

3. Sprinkle the frozen crinkle-cut potatoes over the top of the casserole.

4. Bake in a 350° oven for 45 to 55 minutes or till the fries are golden. Garnish with suggested hamburger toppings, if you like. Makes 8 to 10 servings.

KALBER BAELLELI (SWISS VEAL BALLS)

Doris Streiff of New Glarus, Wisconsin, serves veal, the Swiss mainstay, on special occasions. Substitute lean ground beef in this recipe, if you prefer.

4   eggs
1   cup evaporated milk
1 ½   cups fine, dry bread
     crumbs
½   cup finely chopped onion
½   teaspoon ground nutmeg
2   pounds ground veal
½   pound ground lean pork
     All-purpose flour
1   10¾-ounce can
     condensed cream of
     celery soup
½   cup water

1. Beat eggs slightly. Beat in evaporated milk. Stir in bread crumbs, onion, nutmeg and ½ teaspoon *salt*. Add veal and pork; mix well.

2. Shape the meat mixture into 1½-inch balls. Roll each meatball in the flour. Place meatballs in a 15x10x1-inch baking pan. Bake in a 375° oven for 20 minutes.

3. Using a slotted spoon, transfer meatballs to a 3-quart rectangular baking dish. Stir together celery soup and water till combined. Pour over meatballs in baking dish. Bake, covered, in 375° oven for 20 to 25 minutes. Serves 10.

ARRORSTO VITELLO MAILE (VEAL AND PORK ROAST)

The whole Fontanini family of Highland Park, Illinois, anticipates the holiday meal, featuring Rina Fontanini's pork loin roast wrapped around a veal roast and studded with herbs. The secret of this recipe is not to overcook the meats.

2 2-pound boneless center cut pork-loin roasts
1 ¼-pound boneless veal-loin roast
2 tablespoons snipped fresh rosemary or 2 teaspoons dried, rosemary, crushed
4 large cloves garlic, minced
¼ teaspoon salt
¼ teaspoon pepper
2 tablespoons butter or margarine
1 tablespoon olive oil or cooking oil
½ cup dry white wine

1. Trim excess fat from meats.

2. Combine rosemary, garlic, salt and pepper. Rub veal roast with rosemary mixture to coat. (Rina says she sometimes studs her roast with the tip of a knife and presses the rub inside.)

3. To assemble, place the veal roast between the 2 pork roasts. Tie with string at 1-inch intervals. If necessary, tie 2 strings around lengthwise to hold pieces together. Place in plastic bag and refrigerate roast overnight.

4. In a Dutch oven, brown meat on all sides in hot butter or margarine and olive oil. Add the white wine and cook for 1 to 2 minutes. Remove from heat.

5. Transfer meat to a rack in a shallow roasting pan. Insert meat thermometer. Spoon drippings from Dutch oven over roast. Roast, uncovered, in a 325° oven for 1½ to 1¾ hours or till meat thermometer registers 160°.

6. Transfer roast to a serving platter. Let stand 10 minutes before carving. Serves 12 to 16.

Note: You can use one 5-pound boneless center-cut pork-loin roast or one 5-pound boneless veal-loin roast instead of both. Just rub the meat with the rosemary mixture and roast as directed above.

ITALIAN PORKETTA

This Iron Country recipe comes from Virginia, Minnesota, resident Mary Rosati, who brought it with her from her homeland of Italy.

1 6- to 7-pound fresh pork rump butt or arm picnic roast, skinned and boned
1 teaspoon salt
½ teaspoon pepper
⅓ cup peeled garlic cloves (2 heads)
1 cup fresh fennel greens (tops)
½ teaspoon garlic powder
Italian buns (optional)

1. Unroll pork roast and sprinkle with half the salt and half the pepper.

2. Halve any large cloves of garlic. Arrange garlic, then fennel tops over pork roast. Reroll and tie roast.

3. Sprinkle the outside of the pork roast with remaining salt, pepper and the garlic powder. Place on a rack in a roasting pan. Cover loosely with foil.

4. Bake in a 325° oven for 3¼ to 4 hours or till very tender and meat thermometer inserted in center registers at least 170°. Untie roast and remove fennel tops and garlic, if you like.

5. Slice or shred. Pile on buns, if you like. Makes 8 to 10 servings.

CHERRIES AND CHOPS

Cherries—both tart red and dark sweet—are plentiful during the summer in Michigan and other cherry-growing areas in the Midwest. This enticing dish stars tart red cherries.

6 smoked pork chops, cut ½ inch thick
½ cup sugar
2 teaspoons cornstarch
Dash salt
½ teaspoon finely shredded orange peel
¼ cup orange juice
1½ cups fresh or frozen unsweetened pitted tart red cherries

1. Grill pork chops over *medium* coals for 8 to 10 minutes. Turn and grill for 7 to 8 minutes more or till done.

2. Meanwhile, in a medium saucepan, combine the sugar, cornstarch and salt. Stir in the orange peel, orange juice and cherries. Cook and stir till the sauce is thickened and bubbly. Cook and stir for 2 minutes more.

3. Serve cherry sauce with grilled pork chops. Makes 6 servings.

NUT 'N' CINNAMON PORK

Libbye Hanks of St. Louis, Missouri, was the grand-prize winner of our Pork for All Seasons recipe contest. Libbye says she serves her pork chops over seasoned rice.

6   boneless pork loin chops, 1¼ to 1½ inches thick (about 2 pounds)
1   tablespoon cooking oil
½   cup packed brown sugar
½   cup crème de cassis
½   cup dry white wine
1   tablespoon butter or margarine
2   large red cooking apples, cored and cut into ½-inch wedges
½   cup finely chopped walnuts
    Salt (optional)

1. In a large skillet, brown pork on both sides in hot oil. Arrange browned chops in a 2-quart rectangular baking dish. Season with salt, if you like. Set the browned chops aside.

2. In same skillet, warm brown sugar over medium flame till sugar begins to melt, shaking skillet occasionally to heat sugar evenly. Reduce heat to low and cook till sugar is melted (5 to 7 minutes more). Stir as necessary after brown sugar melts.

3. Carefully stir in crème de cassis (mixture will bubble up and sugar will harden). Cook and stir till mixture is thick and syrupy, and sugar is melted (8 to 10 minutes).

4. Spoon syrup over pork chops. Bake, uncovered, in a 350° oven for 30 to 35 minutes or till meat is tender.

5. Meanwhile, in a saucepan, bring the wine and butter or margarine to boiling; add apple wedges. Return to boiling; reduce heat and simmer, covered, for about 10 minutes or till apples are tender.

6. Arrange the pork chops in a row, overlapping, on a hot platter; sprinkle with walnuts and drizzle with cassis sauce. Arrange the poached apple wedges at the side. Sprinkle with some ground cinnamon. Makes 6 servings.

SWEDISH CHRISTMAS HAM

A dollop of tangy-sweet Mustard Whip adds a suble bite to this ham. The recipe comes from twin sisters Louise Infelt and Gina Suter of Chicago.

1 5- to 7-pound lightly smoked, fully cooked ham
1 egg
1 tablespoon hot-style mustard
Fine, dry bread crumbs
Mustard Whip

1. Trim fat and skin from ham. Place ham on rack in shallow roasting pan.

2. Beat the egg till thick (about 5 minutes). Fold in the mustard; brush over the ham. Sprinkle with some pepper and ¼ to ⅓ cup bread crumbs to coat.

3. Bake in 325° oven for 1½ to 2¼ hours (meat thermometer should read 140°).

4. Prepare Mustard Whip. Serve with sliced ham. Makes 16 to 24 servings.

MUSTARD WHIP: Beat 1 cup *whipping cream* just till soft peaks form. Gently fold in ¼ cup *hot-style mustard* and 1 teaspoon snipped *chives*. Makes 1 cup.

BEER-GLAZED HAM

For the Christmas crowd, North Dakotan Jane Sinner, wife of former Governor George Sinner, bakes a 20-pound ham, then glazes it with this zippy mixture.

1 5- to 7-pound fully cooked boneless ham
¼ cup packed brown sugar
2 tablespoons honey
1 tablespoon beer
1½ teaspoons prepared mustard
Whole cloves (optional)

1. Heat ham according to package directions.

2. Meanwhile, to prepare glaze, combine brown sugar, honey, beer and mustard. Score ham and stud with cloves, if you like. Spoon glaze over ham the last 30 minutes of baking. Makes 14 to 16 servings.

HASH BROWN-HAM CASSEROLE

A savory crust tops this tempting recipe from Joanne Aulenbacher of Shawano, Wisconsin.

1　16-ounce carton dairy
　　sour cream
1　10¾-ounce can
　　condensed cream of
　　chicken soup
1　32-ounce package frozen,
　　loose-pack hash-brown
　　potatoes
2　cups cubed, cooked ham
8　ounces American cheese,
　　cut in cubes (2 cups)
¼　cup chopped onion
　　(optional)
2　cups crushed cornflakes
½　cup butter or margarine
1　cup shredded mozzarella
　　cheese (4 ounces)

1. In a large mixing bowl, combine the dairy sour cream and the condensed cream of chicken soup. Stir in the frozen potatoes, cubed ham, cubed American cheese and chopped onion, if you like.

2. Turn mixture into a 3-quart rectangular baking dish, spreading evenly. Melt butter or margarine. Mix cornflakes and melted butter or margarine. Sprinkle over potato mixture.

3. Bake in a 350° oven for 30 minutes.

4. Sprinkle with mozzarella cheese. Return to oven and bake for 20 to 25 minutes more or till bubbly around the edges and heated through. Makes 8 to 10 servings.

APRICOT-GLAZED CANADIAN BACON

Marilyn Schudy of Kansas City, Missouri, adds a sweet brandy glaze to a dish that she always loved as a youngster. Shop at a meat market for the Canadian bacon.

1　2-pound piece fully
　　cooked Canadian-style
　　bacon
¼　cup packed brown sugar
1　tablespoon apricot
　　brandy
½　teaspoon prepared
　　mustard
　　Canned apricot halves
　　Watercress

1. Score Canadian bacon so the cuts are about 1¼ inches apart. Place on rack in a 13x9x2-inch baking pan. Insert meat thermometer. Bake, uncovered, in 350° oven for 15 minutes.

2. Meanwhile, mix brown sugar, brandy and mustard. Spread some of the glaze on bacon.

3. Bake bacon 15 minutes more or till thermometer registers 140°. Spread bacon with remaining glaze. Garnish with apricot halves and watercress. Slice meat. Serves 8 to 10.

SOUTH-OF-THE-BORDER GRILLED CHICKEN SALAD

Leigh Ann Kloefkorn of Wichita, Kansas, won first place in the Celebrate Kansas Food recipe contest with this surprising salad.

¼ cup soy sauce
¼ cup water
2 tablespoons lime juice (1 lime)
½ teaspoon freshly ground pepper
⅛ teaspoon garlic powder
4 large skinless, boneless chicken breast halves (about 1 pound)
½ cup Glazed Pecans (optional)
2 cups mesquite chips or other wood chips for barbecuing
½ teaspoon freshly ground pepper
8 cups torn mixed salad greens
¾ cup mild salsa
¼ cup buttermilk salad dressing
1 red or green sweet pepper, sliced into thin rings
2 green onions, thinly sliced

1. In a large, shallow container, mix together soy sauce, water, lime juice, ½ teaspoon pepper and garlic powder. Rinse chicken and pat dry. Add to marinade, turning once. Cover; marinate in refrigerator for 6 to 24 hours.

2. Prepare Glazed Pecans, if you like.

3. Soak chips in water for 1 hour. Drain. Add chips to *medium* coals.

4. Grill chicken directly over *medium* coals for 12 to 15 minutes or till done, turning once. Chill chicken.

5. Slice chicken diagonally into bite-size strips. Season with pepper.

6. To assemble salad, on a large platter, layer in order: greens, salsa, salad dressing, pepper rings, chicken, onion and Glazed Pecans, if you like. Makes 4 servings.

GLAZED PECANS: In a small saucepan, combine 1 cup *pecan halves*, ¼ cup *sugar*, 2 tablespoons *water* and ¼ teaspoon *seasoned salt*. Cook and stir over medium-high heat for about 5 minutes or till syrup has changed to crystals and evenly coats the nuts. Spread on a baking sheet. Bake in a 300° oven for 15 minutes or till light brown. Store in an airtight container. Makes 1 cup.

Note: For individual servings: on salad plates, layer ingredients in same order as above.

CHICKEN WITH HORSERADISH CREAM

This zingy, horseradish-sauced chicken dish from Linda Stofleth of Collinsville, Illinois, won raves at Collinsville's International Horseradish Festival.

Horseradish Cream
¼ cup all-purpose flour
1 teaspoon salt
½ teaspoon pepper
4 whole chicken breasts, skinned, boned and halved lengthwise (about 2 pounds)
3 tablespoons butter or margarine
1 clove garlic, minced
1 cup sliced fresh mushrooms
1 cup whipping cream
2 tablespoons snipped parsley
Cooked wild rice

1. Prepare Horseradish Cream.

2. In a plastic bag, combine the flour, salt and pepper. Add half of the chicken breasts and toss to coat. Repeat with remaining chicken.

3. In large skillet, cook coated chicken in melted butter over medium heat for 8 to 10 minutes, turning once. Remove to a heated platter. Keep warm.

4. For sauce, add garlic and mushrooms to drippings in skillet. Cook for 2 minutes. Stir in Horseradish Cream and whipping cream. Bring to boiling. Reduce heat; simmer, uncovered, for 5 minutes. Remove from heat. Stir in snipped parsley.

5. Serve chicken with sauce over wild rice. Makes 8 servings.

HORSERADISH CREAM: Stir together ¼ cup *whipping cream*, 2 tablespoons *mayonnaise* or *salad dressing*, 1 tablespoon *prepared mustard*, 2 tablespoons *prepared horseradish*, ¼ teaspoon *lemon juice*, ¼ teaspoon *Worcestershire sauce*, ⅛ teaspoon *seasoned salt* and a dash *white pepper*. Cover and chill till served.

Nutrition Note: For a calorie-trimmed version of this classy entrée, omit the coating on the chicken and use light mayonnaise in the Horseradish Cream sauce.

CRANBERRY CHICKEN

The Silver Dollar City cooks in Branson, Missouri, invented this colorful holiday chicken dish to serve at one of their restaurants. Guests love it!

3 whole, large chicken breasts, skinned, boned and halved lengthwise
  Onion salt
1 16-ounce can whole cranberry sauce
2 tablespoons butter or margarine, melted
¼ cup fine, dry bread crumbs
¼ cup peanuts, finely chopped
¼ cup sunflower nuts, chopped
2 teaspoons sesame seed
2 teaspoons dried parsley flakes
½ teaspoon paprika
½ teaspoon ground ginger
¼ teaspoon ground red pepper

1. Rinse chicken, then pat dry. Place one chicken piece, boned side up, between 2 pieces of clear plastic wrap. Pound lightly to ¼-inch thickness. Repeat with remaining chicken pieces. Sprinkle lightly with onion salt.

2. Place 1 to 2 tablespoons cranberry sauce in center of each flattened breast. Fold in the sides. Roll up, jelly-roll style. Secure with a toothpick, if necessary. Brush the outside with melted butter.

3. In a medium bowl, combine the bread crumbs, peanuts, sunflower nuts, sesame seeds, parsley, paprika, ginger and red pepper. Roll each chicken bundle in nut mixture to coat.

4. Place chicken in a shallow baking pan or dish. Bake, uncovered, in a 350° oven for 30 to 35 minutes or till done.

5. Meanwhile, in a small saucepan, heat up remaining cranberry sauce. Serve with chicken. Makes 6 servings.

CHICK'S CHICKEN DIVAN

Chick Lillis never expected to fight fires or to don a cook's apron, but she does both at a Madison, Wisconsin, firehouse. Her chicken casserole normally serves 8 to 10—or six hungry Madison firefighters!

1   10-ounce package frozen broccoli spears, thawed

3   medium chicken breasts, skinned, halved lengthwise, boned and cut into bite-size pieces

2   tablespoons butter or margarine

8   ounces fresh mushrooms, sliced

1   10¾-ounce can condensed cream-of-chicken soup

½   cup mayonnaise or salad dressing

⅓   cup chicken broth

1   teaspoon lemon juice

½   teaspoon Worcestershire sauce

¼   teaspoon curry powder

¼   teaspoon dry mustard

1   cup croutons

½   cup shredded cheddar cheese

¼   cup grated Parmesan cheese

    Paprika

1. Arrange the thawed broccoli in the bottom of a 2-quart rectangular baking dish.

2. In a skillet, cook cut-up chicken in butter over medium heat for 6 to 8 minutes or till just done. Add mushrooms; cook for 2 minutes more. Spoon mixture over broccoli.

3. In a saucepan, combine cream-of-mushroom soup, mayonnaise, broth, lemon juice, Worcestershire, curry and dry mustard. Heat through. Pour over chicken mixture.

4. Sprinkle croutons over mixture. Add cheeses. Sprinkle with paprika. Bake in a 350° oven for 30 minutes. Makes 6 servings.

BOW-TIE CHICKEN SALAD

The area near Vincennes, Indiana, is melon-growing country. There, families enjoy wonderful dishes, such as this one, which shows off their home-grown cantaloupe. This recipe is just as tasty when you make it with watermelon.

1   slightly beaten egg
½   cup orange juice
¼   cup honey
3   tablespoons lemon juice
¼   teaspoon ground
      cardamom
2   ounces bow ties or
      wagon-wheel pasta
      (about ¾ cup)
1   small cantaloupe
2   cups cubed, cooked
      chicken or turkey
1   cup seedless grapes,
      halved
½   cup sliced celery
½   cup coarsely chopped
      walnuts

1. For dressing, in saucepan, mix egg, orange juice, honey, lemon juice and cardamom. Cook and stir till slightly thickened and just bubbly. Cool slightly. (Dressing will be thin.)

2. Cook pasta in lightly salted boiling water for 12 to 15 minutes or till just tender. Drain. Rinse with cold water. Drain well.

3. Meanwhile, cut four ½-inch-thick slices from the center of the melon. Peel and seed to form rings of melon. Wrap the rings in clear plastic wrap and refrigerate. Cube enough of the remaining melon to equal 2 cups.

4. In a large bowl, combine the cubed melon, chicken or turkey, grapes, celery, nuts, pasta and dressing. Toss mixture to coat with dressing. Cover and chill for 2 to 24 hours.

5. To serve, arrange the chilled rings of melon on dinner plates. Spoon the chicken-pasta mixture over the rings. Makes 4 servings.

To Use Your Microwave
For dressing, in a microwave-safe 1-quart casserole, combine the egg, orange juice, honey, lemon juice and cardamom. Cover and microcook the mixture on 100% power (high) for 3 to 5 minutes or till slightly thickened and just bubbly, stirring every minute. Cool the slightly. Continue as directed above.

Note: To use watermelon, take a few center slices as directed above, then cut up about 2 cups watermelon to put in the salad.

UNFORGETTABLE CHICKEN PIE

It's attractive, hearty and healthy to eat. Besides that, everyone seems to love this from-scratch, deep-dish chicken hotdish that Rose Nagel of Caledonia, Michigan, bakes up.

½ pound bulk pork sausage
¼ cup butter or margarine
⅓ cup all-purpose flour
½ teaspoon salt
⅛ teaspoon pepper
1 14½-ounce can chicken broth
⅔ cup milk
2 cups chopped cooked chicken or turkey
1 10-ounce package frozen peas, thawed
2 cups all-purpose flour
2 teaspoons celery seed
1 teaspoon paprika
⅔ cup shortening
6 to 7 tablespoons cold water

1. In a large saucepan, brown sausage. Drain off fat and set the pork sausage aside.

2. In the same pan, melt butter or margarine, stir in ⅓ cup flour, *¼ teaspoon* salt and the pepper. Add broth and milk all at once. Cook and stir till thickened and bubbly.

3. Stir in browned sausage, chicken or turkey and thawed peas. Keep warm.

4. Meanwhile, in a medium mixing bowl, prepare crust by combining 2 cups flour, celery seed, paprika and remaining *¼ teaspoon* salt. Cut in the shortening till pieces are the size of small peas. Sprinkle *1 tablespoon* of the water over part of dough mixture, gently toss with fork. Push to side of bowl. Repeat till all is moistened. Divide the dough into thirds. Form ⅔ into a ball and the remaining ⅓ into another ball.

5. On a lightly floured surface, roll the larger ball of dough to about ⅛-inch thickness to fit into a 2-quart round casserole. Ease pastry into the casserole. Trim the pastry to ½ inch beyond the edge of the casserole. For the top crust, roll the smaller ball of dough to about ⅛-inch thickness to fit top of casserole. Cut decorative slits or cutouts so the steam escapes.

6. Transfer the chicken mixture to the pastry-lined casserole. Fold edge of bottom crust over edge of top crust. Flute edge.

7. Bake chicken pie in a 450° oven for 25 to 30 minutes or till the pastry is a golden brown. Makes 6 servings.

GRIDIRON GRILLED TURKEY WITH TOMATO CHUTNEY

Pro-football player and Iowa native Jay Hilgenberg and his wife, Lisa, typically celebrate Christmas Eve with a grilled-turkey feast and presents at the Minneapolis home of Lisa's parents, Layne and Garnett Haugen. You can figure three quarters to one pound of turkey per person—unless you expect a family of hearty-eating Hilgenbergs.

1   cup peeled and chopped
      ripe tomato
1   cup chopped apple
1   cup cider vinegar
½   cup sugar
½   cup peeled and chopped
      green or red tomato
¼   cup chopped green
      pepper
2   tablespoons chopped
      onion
2   teaspoons salt
1½ teaspoons white mustard
      seed
1½ teaspoons celery seed
¼   teaspoon ground ginger
¼   teaspoon ground cloves
¼   teaspoon ground
      cinnamon
1   turkey
    Salt
2   medium onions, sliced
      and separated into
      rings
3   slices white bread
    Greens (optional)
    Sliced orange (optional)

1. To make the tomato chutney, combine ripe tomato, apple, vinegar, sugar, green or red tomato, green pepper, chopped onion, 2 teapoons salt, white mustard seed, celery seed, ginger, cloves and cinnamon in a large saucepan. Bring to boiling. Boil gently about 1 hour or till a thick consistency. Transfer tomato chutney to a covered container and chill. Store in the refrigerator for up to 1 month.

2. Rinse turkey and pat dry with paper toweling. Sprinkle cavities lightly with salt. Place onion rings in body cavity. Close cavity with bread. If opening has a band of skin across the tail, tuck the drumsticks under the band. Or tie legs securely to tail. Twist wing tips under back or tie wing tips up with string.

3. Arrange *medium-hot* coals around drip pan in covered grill. Insert meat thermometer in thigh of turkey. Place turkey on grill above drip pan. Lower hood and grill for 2 to 2½ hours for a 6- to 8-pound turkey or 3½ to 4 hours for a 12- to 16-pound turkey. The turkey is done when the meat thermometer registers 180°.

4. Remove turkey from grill and let stand for 15 minutes before carving. Serve with the tomato chutney. Garnish the platter with greens and sliced orange, if you like. Makes 2 cups tomato chutney.

TURKEY TENDERLOIN WITH GREEN ONIONS

You can bet it's spring in the Midwest when thoughts turn to tender green onions and other early harvest garden vegetables. Use both the onion's green top and slender white bulb in this savory dish.

2 tablespoons cooking oil
1 pound boneless turkey breast tenderloins
2 tablespoons butter or margarine
1 cup ½-inch bias-sliced green onion
1 clove garlic, minced
¼ teaspoon salt
⅛ teaspoon ground red pepper

1. In large skillet, heat cooking oil over medium-high heat. Add turkey; season with salt and pepper. Cook 5 minutes; turn. Reduce heat to medium-low. Cover and cook 15 minutes more. Transfer to a warm platter.

2. In skillet, melt butter. Add onion and garlic. Stir-fry till onion is tender. Add salt and red pepper.

3. Spoon green-onion mixture over cooked turkey breast tenderloins. Makes 4 servings.

LOGGERS' VEGETABLE STUFFING

This stuffing, starring vegetables and nuts, comes from the Minnesota Forest History Center near Grand Rapids, Minnesota.

¾ cup butter
1½ cups shredded carrot
1½ cups shredded parsnip
1 cup chopped onion
1½ teaspoons ground sage
½ teaspoon celery salt
¼ teaspoon pepper
10 cups sourdough or French-bread cubes (about 13 slices, 11 ounces)
¾ cup hazelnuts, walnuts or pecans, toasted and coarsely chopped
¾ to 1 cup water

1. In a skillet melt butter. Add carrot, parsnip, onion, sage, celery salt and pepper. Cook till vegetables are tender, but not brown.

2. Combine bread cubes and nuts. Add vegetable mixture. Drizzle with water; toss. Stuff turkey or bake in casserole, covered, in 325° oven for 45 minutes. Garnish with a carrot curl and celery tops, if you like. Makes 12 cups, enough stuffing for a 12-pound turkey.

CHESTNUT DRESSING

Professional basketball player Bill Laimbeer and the rest of his family all love to dig into this traditional Christmas-dinner dish at Bill's surburban Detroit home.

1 pound chestnuts, roasted, peeled and chopped
1 pound mildly seasoned bulk pork sausage
1 cup finely chopped onion
½ cup hot water
½ cup butter, melted
8 cups dry bread cubes
½ cup snipped fresh parsley
1 teaspoon poultry seasoning
½ teaspoon celery seed
½ teaspoon white pepper
½ teaspoon salt
1 slice bread

1. Slash shells of chestnuts with sharp knife. Roast in a 400° oven for 15 minutes; cool. Peel and coarsely chop chestnuts.

2. Cook sausage and onion till meat is brown, stirring occasionally. Drain off fat. Add hot water and butter. Combine chestnuts, sausage mixture, bread cubes, parsley and seasonings. Toss lightly till bread is moistened. Add ½ cup more hot water, if necessary.

3. Use to stuff a 12-pound turkey. Place bread slice over large cavity to hold stuffing in and prevent overbrowning. Or, place stuffing in a 3-quart rectangular baking dish; cover and bake in a 350° oven for 20 minutes. Uncover; bake for 10 minutes more. Makes 10 cups.

APPLE-APRICOT STUFFING

At the Minnesota Forest History Center near Grand Rapids, Minnesota, visitors share the fun and food of a lumberjack's Christmas feast, including this scrumptious stuffing.

½ cup dried apples, snipped
¼ cup dried apricots, snipped
½ cup chopped onion
½ cup butter, melted
8 cups sourdough, Italian or French bread cubes
¼ cup raisins
1 teaspoon salt
1 teaspoon ground cinnamon
½ teaspoon ground cardamom

1. Pour enough *boiling water* over apples and apricots to cover. Let stand 5 minutes; drain.

2. Cook onion in butter till tender, but not brown. Combine bread, raisins, salt, spices, ⅛ teaspoon *pepper*, drained fruit and onion mixture. Drizzle with enough water to moisten (about ½ cup); toss lightly.

3. Use to stuff a 10-pound turkey. Cover the stuffing in opening of bird with foil to prevent overbrowning. Or, bake the stuffing in a casserole, covered, in a 325° oven for 30 to 35 minutes. Makes 7½ cups.

CYNDI'S SEAFOOD LASAGNA

Owners Benjamin and Cyndi Schultze serve this irresistible blend of shrimp, scallops and crab at The Story Inn restaurant in Story, Indiana.

8   ounces mushrooms
1   tablespoon butter
1   pound fresh spinach, stemmed and chopped
½   of an 8-ounce package cream cheese, softened
8   ounces fresh or frozen shrimp, peeled and deveined
8   ounces fresh or frozen bay scallops
    Bèchamel Sauce (see recipe, page 37)
½   cup chopped shallots or onion
2   large cloves garlic, minced
2   tablespoons olive oil or cooking oil
1   tablespoon dried basil, crushed
1½ teaspoons dried oregano, crushed
¼   cup grated Parmesan cheese
1   to 2 tablespoons dry sherry
7   ounces lasagna noodles (about 9 noodles), cooked, drained and rinsed
4   cups shredded mozzarella cheese (16 ounces)
1   pound crabmeat, cooked and flaked

1. Chop mushrooms. In a large skillet, cook mushrooms in butter for about 8 minutes or till tender and liquid has evaporated. Steam or cook spinach in a small amount of water for 3 to 5 minutes or till just tender. Drain thoroughly. Stir in cream cheese. Set aside.

2. Bring 3 to 4 cups *water* to boiling. Add the shrimp and scallops. Return just to boiling. Drain immediately. Set aside. Prepare the Bechamel Sauce. Cover and keep warm.

3. In a large saucepan, cook shallots and garlic in olive oil till tender. Stir in basil, oregano, ¼ teaspoon *salt* and ⅛ teaspoon *pepper*. Reduce heat to medium low. Add *1½ cups* of the Bechamel Sauce, the Parmesan cheese and sherry. Fold in cooked shrimp and scallops. Remove from heat.

4. To assemble, spread about *½ cup* Bèchamel Sauce in bottom of a greased 3-quart rectangular baking dish. Arrange *3 of the noodles* over the sauce. Spread the shrimp mixture over the noodles; top with *⅓ of the mozzarella*. Arrange *3 more noodles* over mozzarella. Spread spinach mixture over noodles. Top with another *⅓ of the mozzarella*, the mushrooms and crabmeat. Top with remaining noodles. Spread the remaining Bèchamel Sauce over noodles. Cover the baking dish with foil.

5. Bake in a 350° oven for 30 minutes. Remove foil. Sprinkle with the remaining mozzarella cheese. Bake, uncovered, for 15 minutes more or till heated through. Let stand 10 to 15 minutes before serving. Serves 12.

BÈCHAMEL SAUCE

Make this rich sauce to use in Cyndi's Seafood Lasagna on page 36.

⅓ cup butter
⅓ cup all-purpose flour
½ teaspoon salt
⅛ teaspoon white pepper
3 cups milk

1. In a medium saucepan, melt the butter over medium heat. Stir in flour, salt and white pepper. Add milk all at once to the saucepan. Cook and stir the sauce mixture till thickened and bubbly. Cook and stir the mixture for 1 minute more. Makes about 3 cups.

BUTTERMILK-PECAN CATFISH

In scenic Brown County, Indiana, the Story Inn teams up Midwest catfish, pecans and mustard in this tangy main dish.

1 pound fresh or frozen
   catfish fillets
⅔ cup buttermilk
1 tablespoon Dijon-style
   mustard
   Dash paprika
½ cup ground pecans
½ cup all-purpose flour
¼ teaspoon salt
¼ teaspoon white pepper
¼ teaspoon ground nutmeg
2 tablespoons clarified
   butter or olive oil

1. Thaw the catfish fillets, if frozen. Rinse and pat fish dry with paper towels. Cut into serving-size pieces.

2. In a shallow dish, stir together buttermilk, Dijon-style mustard and paprika. Add fish, turning to coat.

3. In another shallow dish, combine ground pecans, flour, salt, pepper and nutmeg. Roll fish in pecan mixture.

4. In a 12-inch skillet, heat clarified butter or olive oil over medium heat. Add fillets. Fry till golden, turning once, for about 7 minutes, adding another tablespoon clarified butter or oil if needed. Makes 4 to 6 servings.

Note: To clarify the butter or margarine, in a small, heavy saucepan, melt the butter or margarine over low heat without stirring. When the butter is completely melted, pour the clear oil layer at the top (the clarified butter or margarine) into a dish. Discard the milky layer.

MONTEREY JACK CHEESE AND EGG CASSEROLE

This rich, cheesy dish from a Missouri reader is oh-so-easy on the cook.

1	4-ounce can chopped green chili peppers
1	16-ounce loaf unsliced French bread
1½	cups shredded Monterey Jack cheese (6 ounces)
1½	cups shredded cheddar cheese (6 ounces)
1	8-ounce package cream cheese, cubed
10	eggs
2	cups milk
½	teaspoon dry mustard
	Dash ground red pepper

1. Drain peppers. Remove crust from bread. Tear bread into chunks (should have 10 cups). In a greased 3-quart rectangular baking dish, arrange bread evenly. Sprinkle with shredded and cream cheeses. Top with peppers.

2. In a large mixing bowl, beat eggs just till mixed. Stir in milk, mustard and red pepper. Pour egg mixture over cheese mixture. Cover and chill for several hours or overnight.

3. Bake, uncovered, in a 350° oven for 55 to 60 minutes or till a knife inserted near the center comes out clean. Let stand for 10 minutes before serving. Makes 12 servings.

EGG-POTATO SCRAMBLE

Janet Pittman of Des Moines fixes this easy-to-make egg dish both at home and over the campfire on weekend camping trips.

8	slices bacon
1½	cups frozen hash brown potatoes with onion and peppers (half of a 24-ounce package)
	Dash salt
	Dash pepper
6	eggs
⅓	cup milk
¼	teaspoon salt
	Dash pepper
½	cup shredded cheddar cheese (2 ounces)

1. In a heavy 10-inch skillet, cook bacon till crisp. Remove and crumble bacon. Pour off all but 2 tablespoons fat. Add potatoes to skillet. Sprinkle with dash of salt and pepper. Cook and stir till potatoes are light-brown.

2. Meanwhile, beat together eggs, milk, ¼ teaspoon salt and dash pepper. Pour over potatoes. Cook without stirring till mixture begins to set on bottom and around edges. Using spatula, lift and fold partially cooked eggs so uncooked portion flows underneath. Continue cooking over medium heat about 4 minutes or till eggs are cooked but still glossy and moist.

3. Sprinkle with bacon and cheese. Serves 4.

SOUPS
AND
STEWS

*Illinois
Corn-Sausage
Chowder*

Iowa Steak Soup

SOUPS AND STEWS

EAGLE HARBOR INN'S HERBED TOMATO SOUP

Ladles in hand, the cooks from Michigan's Upper Peninsula challenge some of the Midwest's snowiest weather with soups of all kinds. Besides ice fishing and snowmobiling, creating hearty soups is one more way "Yoopers" (as Upper Peninsula residents are called) welcome winter. At Eagle Harbor Inn, near the tip of the Keweenaw Peninsula, soup-maker Mary Probst fights the chill with this creation, brimming with vegetables.

1 medium unpeeled potato, chopped
1 medium onion, chopped
1 stalk celery, chopped
1 clove garlic, minced
2 tablespoons butter or margarine
2 tablespoons water
2 cups tomato juice
2 cups milk
1 10¾-ounce can condensed tomato soup
2 tablespoons snipped fresh parsley
½ teaspoon garlic powder
½ teaspoon dried thyme, crushed
¼ teaspoon pepper

1. In a large saucepan, cook the potato, onion, celery and garlic in butter or margarine and 2 tablespoons water, covered, for 8 to 10 minutes or till vegetables are tender.

2. Stir in the tomato juice, milk, soup, parsley, garlic powder, thyme and pepper.

3. Heat through. Makes 5 side-dish servings.

ALL-AMERICAN CHEESE SOUP

Feature this versatile soup from Randy Laferriere of Springfield, Missouri, with sandwiches for supper or as an appetizing first course.

¼ cup finely chopped onion
¼ cup finely chopped carrot
¼ cup finely chopped celery
2 tablespoons butter
⅓ cup all-purpose flour
2 cups chicken broth
2 cups light cream
8 ounces sharp process
  American cheese,
  shredded
Ground red pepper

1. In large saucepan, cook vegetables in butter till tender, but not brown.

2. Stir flour into broth till smooth. Add broth and cream to vegetables; cook and stir till thickened and bubbly.

3. Add cheese. Season with red pepper, salt and pepper. Cook and stir till cheese is melted and soup is heated through. Makes 8 servings as a starter, 4 servings as a main course.

SCHLÖEGEL'S CABBAGE SOUP

Schlöegel's Bay View Restaurant in Menominee, Michigan, teams up nine ingredients in this hearty soup. Serve a big bowl as a main dish or a small bowl on the side.

1 small onion, chopped
  (⅓ cup)
1 stalk celery, sliced
  (½ cup)
¼ cup butter or margarine
½ cup all-purpose flour
8 cups chicken broth or
  chicken stock
4 cups shredded cabbage
8 to 12 ounces fully cooked
  Polish sausage, halved
  lengthwise and thinly
  sliced
2 teaspoons snipped fresh
  parsley
½ teaspoon white pepper

1. In a 4-quart Dutch oven, cook the chopped onion and the sliced celery in the butter or margarine till the vegetables are tender, but not browned.

2. Stir the all-purpose flour into the vegetables in the Dutch oven till the mixture is smooth. Stir in the chicken broth or chicken stock. Add the shredded cabbage. Cook and stir till the soup mixture is thickened and bubbly. Reduce the heat. Simmer the soup mixture, uncovered, for about 3 minutes.

3. Stir the Polish sausage, parsley and white pepper into the simmering soup. Cook, uncovered, for 2 minutes more. Makes 10 side-dish servings or 6 main-dish servings (with the 12 ounces of cooked sausage).

VEGETABLE VOMACKA

This tasty soup comes from historic Schumacher's New Prague Hotel in New Prague, Minnesota. John and Kathleen Schumacher point out that it tastes best in summer, when you make it with fresh garden vegetables. They suggest, "Let your imagination go and add all sorts of different vegetables."

2 tablespoons butter or margarine
½ cup chopped onion
½ cup chopped carrot
½ cup chopped celery
2 cloves garlic, minced
2 tablespoons all-purpose flour
3 cups chicken stock or broth
1 tablespoon instant chicken bouillon granules
1 teaspoon dried dillweed
1½ teaspoons pickling spice
¼ teaspoon black peppercorns
1½ cups fresh or frozen cut green beans
1½ cups peeled, diced potato
1 cup whipping cream
2 to 3 teaspoons cider vinegar

1. In a heavy, large kettle or Dutch oven, melt the butter or margarine. Add the chopped onion, carrot, celery and garlic. Cook and stir over medium-high heat till the vegetables are tender, but not brown.

2. Reduce heat. Stir in the flour. Cook, stirring constantly, over medium heat for 2 minutes. *Do not brown.*

3. Stir in chicken stock or broth, bouillon granules and dillweed. Tie pickling spice and black peppercorns in a cheesecloth bag. Add to soup. Bring to a slow, rolling boil. Reduce heat. Cover and simmer for 20 minutes. (If using fresh beans, add them to the kettle after 10 minutes of simmering. Cover and simmer for 10 minutes more.)

4. Add frozen beans and potato. Return to boiling; reduce heat. Simmer for about 15 minutes or till potato and beans are tender.

5. Remove pickling spice bag. Slowly stir cream into soup. Stir in vinegar. Makes 5 or 6 side-dish servings.

Note: The Schumachers advise that if this soup is too thin for you, you may thicken it with ¼ cup all-purpose flour mixed with ¼ cup milk. You also can add cooked veal, beef, venison, rabbit and/or squirrel to make a booya-style soup.

ELLA'S MATZO BALL SOUP

At Ella's Kosher Deli and Ice Cream Parlor in Madison, Wisconsin, they make matzo balls the Old Country way—big and firm. Try a bowl or two of this soup. As Grandma used to say, "It couldn't hurt."

4 slightly beaten eggs
2 tablespoons melted chicken fat or cooking oil (if you make your own chicken broth, skim that fat and use it here)
1 cup matzo meal
½ teaspoon salt
¼ teaspoon pepper
⅓ cup chicken broth
2 to 3 quarts water
5 cups chicken broth
   Snipped fresh parsley (optional)

1. In a mixing bowl, beat together the eggs, chicken fat, matzo meal, salt and pepper. Stir in the ⅓ cup chicken broth. Cover; refrigerate for 1 hour so the matzo can absorb the broth.

2. Place water in a large saucepan or Dutch oven; bring to boiling. Using wet hands, shape matzo mixture into 5 balls (about 2½ inches in diameter) and drop into boiling water. Reduce heat and simmer, covered, for 12 to 15 minutes or till done.

3. Meanwhile, heat up the 5 cups chicken broth. Using a slotted spoon, remove the matzo balls from the kettle and place one in each of 5 bowls of broth. Top with parsley, if you like. Makes 5 side-dish servings.

SHIRLEY'S IOWA CORN CHOWDER

Edna Yoder of Iowa City, Iowa, shared this hearty soup with Shirley Fry, wife of University of Iowa football coach Hayden Fry. It's an update of an Amish favorite.

5 slices bacon
1 medium onion, sliced and separated into rings
2½ cups milk
2 cups frozen corn (1 10-ounce package)
1 10¾-ounce can condensed cream of mushroom soup
1 cup diced potato, cooked

1. In a large saucepan, cook bacon till crisp. Remove; drain on paper towels. Crumble bacon. Reserve 2 to 3 tablespoons drippings in the saucepan.

2. Cook onion rings in reserved drippings till tender. Stir in the milk, corn, soup and potato.

3. Bring mixture to boiling. Reduce heat and simmer for 2 to 3 minutes. Remove from heat. Season to taste with salt. Top each bowl of chowder with some of the crumbled bacon. Makes 4 to 6 side-dish servings.

RYAN'S REVENGE CHILI

From Murphysboro, Illinois, John Ryan's spicy prizewinner goes well with crusty bread. If you can't find Mexican oregano, substitute regular dried oregano.

3½ pounds boneless beef chuck
2 pounds pork sirloin
3 12-ounce cans of beer
½ cup and 3 tablespoons chili powder
¼ cup ground cumin
2 tablespoons paprika
4 teaspoons beef bouillon granules
1 tablespoon dried Mexican oregano, crushed
4 pounds coarse-ground beef chuck
1 tablespoon cooking oil
4 medium onions, chopped
3 Anaheim chili peppers, seeded and chopped
10 cloves garlic, minced
1 8-ounce can tomato sauce
2 tablespoons ground coriander
2 tablespoons green chili sauce
1 tablespoon mole poblano (look for it in the Mexican-food section of large supermarkets)
1 tablespoon sugar
2 tablespoons lime juice
   Shredded Monterey Jack cheese

1. Cut boneless beef chuck and pork sirloin into ½-inch cubes. In a Dutch oven, combine 2½ cups *water*, beer, chili powder, cumin, paprika, bouillon granules and oregano. Bring to boiling.

2. Meanwhile, in skillet, brown meats in small batches. Drain off fat. Add meats to liquid in Dutch oven. Add ½ teaspoon *salt* and ½ teaspoon *pepper*.

3. In the skillet, heat cooking oil. Add onions, chili peppers and garlic. Cook till tender. Add to mixture in Dutch oven.

4. To chili mixture, stir in tomato sauce, coriander, chili sauce, mole poblano and sugar. Return to boiling. Reduce heat. Cover and simmer for 2 hours.

5. Stir in lime juice. Top with Monterey Jack cheese. Makes 8 to 10 servings.

Note: The volatile oils in chili peppers can burn your skin and eyes, so avoid touching the peppers unless you're wearing plastic or rubber gloves. If your skin touches the peppers, wash well with some soap and water.

SCREAMIN' MIMI'S GOURMET CHILI

Suzy and Boadie Hoy of St. Marys, Ohio, suggest complementing this spicy-hot sizzler with a glass of cabernet sauvignon.

1   pound ground beef
½   pound bacon, cut into bite-size pieces
1   teaspoon crushed red pepper
3   pounds beef round steak, cubed
6   cloves garlic, minced
1   large onion, chopped
1   stalk celery, chopped
2   sweet red peppers, chopped
1   12-ounce can beer
⅓   cup chili powder
2   tablespoons ground cumin
2   teaspoons ground red pepper
1   teaspoon dried Mexican oregano or regular oregano, crushed
1   14-ounce can chicken broth
1   14-ounce can beef broth
1   12-ounce can tomato juice
2   tablespoons lemon juice or lime juice
2   tablespoons molasses
2   tablespoons vinegar
2   tablespoons Masa Harina (optional)

1. In a large kettle or Dutch oven, cook ground beef till brown. Drain off fat. Remove meat and set aside.

2. Add bacon and crushed red pepper to kettle. Cook bacon till crisp. Remove bacon and drain on paper towels, leaving bacon drippings in kettle.

3. Cook steak, half at a time, in bacon fat till meat is brown. Drain off fat. Return all meat to kettle.

4. Stir in the garlic, onion, celery and red peppers. Stir in beer, chili powder, cumin, red pepper and oregano. Bring mixture to boiling. Reduce heat. Cover; simmer for 10 minutes.

5. Add chicken broth, beef broth, tomato juice, lemon juice, molasses, vinegar, beef and bacon. Stir in Masa Harina, if you like. Bring to boiling. Reduce heat. Cover; simmer for 2 to 3 hours. Makes 10 servings.

LYNNE'S CINCINNATI CHILI

A Cincinnati friend, Lynne Rempe, sent us this recipe for Cincinnati's unique chili that's traditionally served over spaghetti. She and her fellow cooks say it's the best make-at-home recipe they've tried.

4 cups water
2 8-ounce cans tomato
   sauce
2 cups chopped onion
2 tablespoons chili powder
2 tablespoons vinegar
2 teaspoons Worcestershire
   sauce
2 teaspoons ground
   cinnamon
1 teaspoon salt
1 teaspoon cumin
½ teaspoon ground allspice
¼ teaspoon ground cloves
¼ teaspoon garlic powder
½ ounce unsweetened
   chocolate
1 bay leaf
1 dried red chili pepper
2 pounds lean ground beef
   Hot cooked spaghetti
   Chopped onion
   (optional)
   Shredded cheese
   (optional)
   Canned kidney beans,
   rinsed and drained
   (optional)

1. In a 4-quart Dutch oven, combine water, tomato sauce, 2 cups chopped onion, chili powder, vinegar, Worcestershire sauce, cinnamon, salt, cumin, allspice, cloves, garlic powder, unsweetened chocolate, bay leaf and chili pepper; bring to boiling.

2. Crumble ground beef and add slowly to boiling liquid; return to boiling.

3. Reduce heat and simmer for 2 to 3 hours, uncovered, till thickened as desired. Remove bay leaf and chili pepper.

4. Serve over spaghetti. Top with additional chopped onion, shredded cheese and/or kidney beans, if you like. Makes about 5 cups.

HEARTY BUFFET CHILI

Laura Braun of Filion, Michigan, ladles this mellow, satisfying winner over rice. Then, she adds lots of toppings.

1   pound ground beef
⅓   cup chopped onion
1   clove garlic, minced
1   16-ounce can whole tomatoes, cut up
1   15-ounce can tomato sauce
2   teaspoons chili powder
1   teaspoon salt
½   teaspoon crushed red pepper
¼   teaspoon pepper
1   15¾-ounce can kidney beans in chili sauce
1   to 2 cups cooked rice
1   cup shredded Monterey Jack or cheddar cheese (4 ounces)
½   cup chopped onion (optional)
½   cup dairy sour cream (optional)

1. In a large saucepan, cook beef, ⅓ cup onion and garlic till beef is brown and onion is tender. Drain off fat.

2. Stir *undrained* tomatoes, tomato sauce, chili powder, salt, crushed red pepper and pepper into browned meat in saucepan. Bring to boiling. Reduce heat. Cover; simmer for 1 hour.

3. Add beans with chili sauce to saucepan. Cover; simmer for 30 minutes.

4. In small individual bowls, set out remaining ingredients for guests or family members to serve themselves. For a serving, place some of the cooked rice in a soup bowl. Top with chili mixture, then cheese, then onion and some sour cream, if you like. Makes 4 to 6 servings.

IOWA STEAK SOUP

Cynthia Kenyon of Cedar Falls, Iowa, says this spiced-up version of a Midwest classic is her family's all-time favorite.

1 cup chopped onion
1 cup chopped carrot
1 cup chopped celery
1 cup water
4 teaspoons beef bouillon granules
2 pounds ground beef round or beef round steak, cut into strips or cubes
1 tablespoon cooking oil (optional)
¼ teaspoon garlic powder
½ teaspoon salt
¾ cup butter
1 cup all-purpose flour
1 10-ounce package frozen mixed vegetables
1 7½-ounce can tomatoes, cut up
2 tablespoons snipped fresh parsley
2 teaspoons Kitchen Bouquet
1 to 2 teaspoons dried basil, crushed
1 teaspoon pepper

1. In saucepan, bring onion, carrot, celery and water to boiling; reduce heat, cover and cook for 1 minute. Drain vegetables, reserving liquid. Add bouillon granules to liquid; set aside. Set vegetables aside.

2. In large kettle or Dutch oven, brown meat, half at a time. (If using steak, cook in 1 tablespoon cooking oil.) Drain. Remove meat from kettle. Add garlic powder and salt. Set meat mixture aside.

3. In same kettle, melt butter; whisk in flour. Add enough water to reserved liquid to make 8 cups. Stir into butter mixture all at once. Cook and stir till thickened and bubbly. Add frozen mixed vegetables, *undrained* tomatoes, parsley, Kitchen Bouquet, basil, pepper, reserved vegetables and cooked meat. Cook, stirring occasionally, till soup is heated through. Makes 8 servings.

CHEESY BRAT STEW

This hearty sausage stew from Sharon Pappenfuss of Appleton, Wisconsin, was a prizewinner in our Heavenly Hotdishes contest. It features an all-star lineup of ingredients from Sharon's home state.

6 fully cooked bratwurst or
   Polish sausage,
   (1 pound)
4 medium potatoes,
   cooked, peeled and
   cubed
1 16-ounce can cut green
   beans, drained
1 10¾-ounce can
   condensed cream of
   mushroom soup
1 cup shredded cheddar
   cheese (4 ounces)
1 small onion, chopped

1. Cut bratwurst or Polish sausage into ½-inch pieces. In a 3-quart round casserole, stir together the bratwurst or Polish sausage, potatoes, green beans, cream of mushroom soup, cheddar cheese and chopped onion.

2. Bake the casserole, covered, in a 350° oven for about 45 minutes or till heated through. Makes 8 servings.

ILLINOIS CORN-SAUSAGE CHOWDER

Debbie Vanni of Libertyville, Illinois, started soup making at the tender age of 8. Sausage adds a savory new twist to her celebrated corn chowder.

1 pound bulk pork sausage
1 cup coarsely chopped
   onion
4 cups ½-inch cubes peeled
   potato
½ teaspoon dried
   marjoram, crushed
1 17-ounce can cream-style
   corn
1 17-ounce can whole
   kernel corn, drained
1 12-ounce can evaporated
   milk

1. In a Dutch oven or kettle, cook sausage and onion till sausage is brown and onion is tender; drain on paper towels.

2. Return cooked sausage and onion to Dutch oven with potato cubes, marjoram, 2 cups *water*, 1 teaspoon *salt* and ⅛ teaspoon *freshly ground pepper*. Bring to boiling; reduce heat and simmer just till potato cubes are tender, about 15 minutes.

3. Add cream-style corn, whole kernel corn and evaporated milk. Heat through. Serves 6.

HARVEST BEAN SOUP

Bean soups abound at food stands during the New Albany, Indiana, Harvest Home-coming festival. Here's a version, that combines the best of all the soups we sampled.

½ pound dry great northern beans or navy beans

4 ounces fully cooked ham or fully cooked lean turkey sausage, cut into bite-size pieces

2 medium carrots, chopped

1 medium potato, chopped

½ cup chopped onion

½ teaspoon dried oregano, crushed

¼ teaspoon dried sage, crushed

2 cups milk

1. Rinse beans. In a 4-quart Dutch oven or large saucepan, combine beans and enough water to cover. Bring to boiling. Reduce heat and simmer for 2 minutes. Remove from heat. Cover and let stand for 1 hour. Drain.

2. Stir ham or sausage, carrots, potatoes, onion, oregano, sage, 3½ cups *water*, 1 teaspoon *salt* and ¼ teaspoon *pepper* into beans. Bring to boiling. Reduce heat. Cover and simmer for 2 to 2½ hours or till beans are tender, adding more water, if necessary.

3. Stir in milk. Heat through, stirring occasionally. Season to taste. Makes 6 servings.

MICHIGAN NAVY BEAN AND POTATO SOUP

Irene Johnson's family farms in the "thumb" of Michigan, a region famous for growing navy beans. This satisfying bean recipe was first prepared by Irene's mother-in-law.

2 cups dry navy beans

2 cups chopped, peeled potatoes

1 cup chopped onion

½ cup coarsely shredded carrot

1 tablespoon ketchup

1 teaspoon salt

⅛ teaspoon pepper

1 (or more) cups chopped ham (optional)

1. Rinse beans. In a 4-quart Dutch oven or large saucepan, combine beans and enough water to cover. Cover pan; let stand overnight. (Or, prepare beans as in step 1 of recipe above). Drain.

2. Add 7½ cups fresh water. Bring to boiling; reduce heat and cook, covered, over medium heat for 1 hour or till beans are nearly tender.

3. Add remaining ingredients. (Omit salt, if ham is added to the soup.) Return to boiling; reduce heat. Simmer for 30 minutes or till beans and vegetables are tender. Mash beans and vegetables slightly, if you like. Serves 8.

HERNEKEITTO (FINNISH SPLIT-PEA SOUP)

Aune Kangas shares the foods of her Finnnish heritage with visitors to Ironworld USA near Chisholm, Minnesota. As Aune explains Finnish customs, she fills vistors' bowls with this hearty soup—full of ham, carrots, onion and potatoes.

5 whole allspice
6 cups water
2 cups dried yellow or
    green split peas
2 cups cubed fully cooked
    ham or 1½ pounds
    smoked pork hocks
2 cups cubed potatoes
1 cup chopped carrots
1 small onion, chopped
¼ teaspoon salt
    Dash pepper

1. Wrap allspice in cheesecloth and tie with string to form a spice bag. In a large saucepan, combine water, peas, ham or pork hocks and allspice. Bring to boiling. Reduce heat. Cover and simmer for 1 hour.

2. Add remaining ingredients. Return to boiling. Reduce heat. Cover; simmer 30 minutes.

3. Remove spice bag. If using pork hocks, remove and cool slightly. When cool enough to handle, remove meat from bones and coarsely chop. Discard bones. Return meat to soup. Makes 8 to 10 servings.

ERWTENSOEP (DUTCH SPLIT-PEA SOUP)

This soup is part of the Dutch hertiage in communities throughout the Heartland.

2¼ cups dry, green split peas
    (1 pound), rinsed
8 cups water
2 pounds smoked pork
    hocks
½ pound slab bacon, diced
3 leeks, sliced
1 medium onion, chopped
3 medium potatoes, peeled
    and diced
1 cup chopped celery
12 ounces fully cooked
    smoked sausage

1. In a Dutch oven or kettle, combine peas, water, pork hocks, bacon, leeks and onion. Bring to boiling; reduce heat. Skim off foam. Cover; simmer 1 hour, stirring occasionally.

2. Remove pork hocks. Cool slightly. When cool enough to handle, remove and discard skin and bones. Chop meat; return to soup with potatoes and celery. Bring to boiling. Reduce heat; simmer 10 minutes.

3. Slice sausage ¼-inch thick. Add sausage to soup. Season with *pepper*. Heat through. Makes 8 servings.

WHITE SURPRISE CHILI

From Villa Park, Illinois, Denise Smelter's chili looks like navy bean soup, but tastes like mild chicken chili—a true culinary surprise.

1   **pound dry great northern beans**
6   **cups water**
6   **cups chicken broth**
1   **large onion, chopped (1 cup)**
2   **cloves garlic, minced**
2   **4-ounce cans diced green chili peppers**
1   **tablespoon dried oregano, crushed**
1   **tablespoon ground cumin**
½   **teaspoon ground red pepper**
½   **teaspoon salt**
½   **teaspoon pepper**
4   **cups chopped, cooked chicken**
½   **cup shredded Monterey Jack cheese (2 ounces)**
    Sliced fresh chili peppers (optional)

1. Rinse great northern beans. Place in a Dutch oven and add water. Bring to boiling. Reduce heat and simmer, uncovered, for 2 minutes. Remove from heat. Cover and let beans soak for 1 hour. (Or, cover and soak the beans overnight.) Drain off water.

2. In the same Dutch oven, combine the great northern beans, broth, onion, garlic, chilies, oregano, cumin, red pepper, salt and pepper. Bring to boiling. Reduce heat. Cover and simmer for 1 hour.

3. Stir in the cooked chicken and simmer, covered, for ½ to 1 hour more. Before serving, stir in the shredded cheese just till melted. Serve with additional cheese and sliced chili peppers, if you like. Makes 5 to 6 servings.

Note: For broth and cooked chicken, in a large Dutch oven, combine two 3-pound *broiler-fryer chickens*, cut up, and enough water to cover (about 6 cups). Add ½ teaspoon *salt*. Bring to boiling. Reduce heat. Cover and simmer for about 1 hour or till chicken is tender. Remove chicken, reserving broth. Let chicken stand till cool enough to handle. Remove the chicken meat and discard the skin and bones.

Store chicken and broth separately in tightly covered containers in the refrigerator. Lift fat from broth when well-chilled, or skim fat from hot broth. Broth and chicken can be frozen (freeze a 4-cup portion of the chicken for the chili). Makes 6 cups broth and 6 cups cooked chicken.

VIERLING SALOON'S CREAM OF CHICKEN SOUP WITH WILD RICE

Chef Eileen McGreevy's hearty chicken soup has become a house specialty at the Vierling Saloon and Sample Room in Marquette, Michigan.

8 ounces uncooked wild rice (1 ⅓ cups)

1 3- to 3½-pound broiler-fryer chicken, cut up

7 cups water

12 ounces sliced mushrooms (4½ cups)

2 tablespoons cooking oil

1 cup chopped onion

1 cup chopped celery

2 tablespoons instant chicken bouillon granules

¾ teaspoon white pepper

½ teaspoon salt

½ cup butter or margarine

¾ cup all-purpose flour

4 cups milk

¾ cup dry white wine

1. Cook wild rice according to package directions for 30 minutes; drain off liquid. Set partially cooked rice aside.

2. In a 5- or 6-quart Dutch oven, combine the chicken and water. Bring to boiling. Reduce heat. Cover and simmer for 35 to 40 minutes or till chicken is tender.

3. Remove chicken from broth and let stand till cool enough to handle. Skim fat from broth. Strain and reserve broth. Remove chicken meat from bones. Cut into bite-size pieces.

4. In the same Dutch oven, cook mushrooms in hot oil for 4 to 5 minutes or till tender. Add onion and celery. Cover and cook for 5 to 10 minutes or till tender, stirring once. Remove from heat. Return broth to Dutch oven.

5. Add the partially cooked wild rice to chicken broth. Stir in the bouillon granules, white pepper and salt. Bring to boiling. Reduce heat and simmer, uncovered, for 15 minutes.

6. In a large saucepan, melt the butter. Stir in flour till smooth. Add milk all at once. Cook and stir till bubbly. Stir into soup mixture.

7. Stir in chicken and wine. Heat through. Makes 8 servings.

FISH CHOWDER WITH LEEKS

Tailgate parties in Midwest states from Ohio to Kansas often feature hearty, warming soups such as this one to help football fans ward off blustery game-day winds.

1 pound fresh or frozen boned and skinned northern or walleye pike, lake trout or lake perch fillets

1½ cups water

1 cup clam juice or fish stock

2 medium potatoes, peeled and diced

1 stalk celery, coarsely chopped

1 medium bay leaf

3 slices bacon

1 medium leek, cut into ¼-inch slices

½ cup coarsely chopped onion

3 cups light cream

¼ cup all-purpose flour

2 teaspoons finely snipped fresh parsley

¼ teaspoon salt

¼ teaspoon dried oregano, crushed

¼ teaspoon dried thyme, crushed

¼ teaspoon pepper
Several dashes bottled hot pepper sauce
Butter
Leek slices

1. Thaw fish, if frozen; cut into ½-inch pieces.

2. In a Dutch oven, combine water, clam juice or fish stock, potatoes and celery. Bring to boiling; cover and simmer for 5 minutes. Stir in fish and bay leaf. Cover and simmer for 5 to 10 minutes or till fish is tender.

3. Meanwhile, in a skillet, cook bacon till crisp. Drain, reserving 2 tablespoons of the bacon drippings in the skillet. Crumble bacon and set aside.

4. In skillet, cook leek and onion in drippings until tender but not brown.

5. Blend *1 cup* of the cream into the flour. Stir into fish mixture; add bacon, leek mixture, parsley, salt, oregano, thyme, pepper, hot pepper sauce and remaining cream. Cook and stir chowder till bubbly; cook for 2 minutes more. Remove bay leaf. Dot chowder with butter. Garnish with leek slices. Makes 8 servings.

VIERLING SALOON'S SPINACH-LENTIL SOUP

Here's a low-fat, meatless soup that warms Marquette, Michigan, diners at the Vierling Saloon on cold January days. It's spiced with mustard seed, coriander and lemon.

1	cup uncooked lentils
2	10-ounce packages frozen chopped spinach
3	tablespoons cooking oil
1	teaspoon mustard seed
1	small onion, chopped
4	cups chicken broth
4	teaspoons lemon juice
2	teaspoons white pepper
¾	teaspoon ground coriander
4	ounces cheddar cheese

1. Cook lentils according to package directions. Thaw frozen spinach. Set aside.

2. In a large saucepan, heat cooking oil over medium heat. Add mustard seed and let cook for 1 to 2 minutes or till seeds pop.

3. Add onion and cook till tender.

4. Add spinach, broth, lemon juice, pepper and coriander. Stir in lentils. Heat through. Top with cheese. Serves 4 to 6.

TIMBER CHARLIE'S CHEESY POTATO SOUP

This flavorful soup comes from Charlie Autterson's restaurant in Newberry, Michigan.

6	medium potatoes
1	small onion
1	stalk celery, chopped
1	small carrot, chopped
2	tablespoons butter or margarine
2	tablespoons cornstarch
8	cups milk
2	tablespoons instant chicken bouillon granules
4	cups shredded American cheese (16 ounces)
1½	cups chopped fully cooked ham (8 ounces)

1. Peel and cube potatoes. In a large saucepan, combine potatoes with enough water to cover. Bring to boiling and cook, covered, for about 12 minutes or till potatoes are tender. Drain.

2. In a 4-quart Dutch oven, cook onion, celery and carrot in butter till tender. Stir in cornstarch. Add milk and bouillon granules to the cooked onion mixture. Stir in potatoes.

3. Cook and stir till slightly thickened. Cook and stir for 2 minutes more.

4. Stir in the cheese till melted. Stir in the ham. Heat through. Serve topped with additional cheese, if you like. Serves 8 to 10.

SIDE DISHES

Cheddary Asparagus Spoon Bread

Microwave Asparagus with Hollandaise

SIDE DISHES

CHEDDARY ASPARAGUS SPOON BREAD

True to its name, this soufflélike side dish needs a spoon for serving. It's just one of the creative ways Midwesterners enjoy asparagus.

2 cups fresh asparagus cut into ½-inch pieces
1½ cups milk
½ cup cornmeal
2 cups shredded cheddar cheese (8 ounces)
1 tablespoon butter or margarine
1½ teaspoons baking powder
1 teaspoon sugar
¼ teaspoon salt
4 egg yolks
4 egg whites

1. In a saucepan, cook asparagus in a small amount of boiling water for 5 to 6 minutes or till just tender. Drain well.

2. In a medium saucepan, combine milk and cornmeal. Cook, stirring constantly, over medium-high heat till thickened and bubbly.

3. Remove saucepan from heat. Stir in the cheese, butter or margarine, baking powder, sugar and salt. Beat with a whisk or wooden spoon till the shredded cheese is melted.

4. Beat egg yolks, one at a time, into cheese mixture till combined.

5. In a small mixer bowl, beat egg whites with an electric mixer till stiff peaks form (tips stand straight).

6. Fold egg whites into yolk mixture till combined. Gently fold in the asparagus. Turn the fluffy asparagus mixture into an ungreased 2-quart round casserole or soufflé dish.

7. Bake in a 350° oven for 45 to 60 minutes or till a knife inserted near the center comes out clean. Eat at once. Makes 6 to 8 servings.

MICROWAVE ASPARAGUS WITH HOLLANDAISE

Michigan is one of the top asparagus-growing states in the nation. No matter where you get your asparagus, this lemony sauce is a great way to dress it up.

1½ **pounds fresh asparagus spears, washed and woody bases discarded**
2 **tablespoons water**
3 **beaten egg yolks**
1 **tablespoon water**
1 **tablespoon fresh lemon juice**
 Dash salt
 Dash white pepper
½ **cup butter or margarine, cut into thirds and brought to room temperature**

1. In a microwave-safe 1½-quart rectangular baking dish, arrange asparagus with tips toward the center. Add the 2 tablespoons water. Cover the baking dish with vented microwave-safe clear plastic wrap. Microcook the asparagus on 100% power (high) for 9 to 11 minutes or till crisp-tender, turning the baking dish once. Drain and keep warm.

2. Meanwhile, for hollandaise sauce: In top of a double boiler, combine yolks, 1 tablespoon water, lemon juice, salt and pepper. Add one piece of the butter. Place over boiling water (upper pan shouldn't touch water). Cook, stirring rapidly, till the butter melts and the sauce begins to thicken. Add remaining butter, a piece at a time, stirring constantly. Cook and stir till thicker (1 to 2 minutes). Immediately remove from heat. If sauce is too thick or curdles, immediately beat in 1 to 2 tablespoons hot tap water. Serve over asparagus. Serves 6.

SWEET-POTATO SALAD

Jack and Mary's place at Branson, Missouri's Silver Dollar City serves this unique salad.

6 **medium sweet potatoes, peeled**
1 **8-ounce can pineapple chunks, drained**
½ **cup sliced celery**
½ **cup chopped pecans**
1 **cup mayonnaise or salad dressing**
¼ **cup dairy sour cream**

1. In a large saucepan, cook sweet potatoes in boiling water for 25 to 35 minutes or till tender. Let cool, then cut into ¾-inch cubes.

2. In a large bowl, combine the sweet potatoes, pineapple, celery and pecans.

3. Combine mayonnaise or salad dressing and sour cream. Fold into salad. Chill, if you like. Makes 8 servings.

TAILGATE POTATO SALAD

No matter what Midwest team you're cheering for, this tasty salad is sure to be a hit at your pregame (or any other) party.

1 cup fresh cut green beans or 1 cup frozen cut green beans
1 pound whole small potatoes
¾ cup crumbled feta cheese (3 ounces)
¾ cup sliced olives
⅓ cup coarsely chopped green onion
¼ cup coarsely chopped green pepper
2 tablespoons large capers, drained (optional)
  Herb Dressing or ½ cup bottled herb dressing
¾ cup sliced radishes

1. In a large covered saucepan, cook fresh beans in lightly salted boiling water for 10 minutes. Add potatoes; return to boiling. Cook 10 to 15 minutes more or till vegetables are tender. Drain. (If using frozen green beans, add to boiling potatoes the last 5 minutes of cooking.) Drain and cool. Quarter potatoes.

2. In a large bowl, combine potatoes, beans, cheese, olives, green onion, pepper and capers, if you like. Pour Dressing over salad; toss lightly to coat. Cover and chill salad for several hours or overnight.

3. Before serving or transporting, stir in radishes. To take to a tailgate party, pack in cooler with ice. Makes 8 servings.

HERB DRESSING: In a bowl, combine ⅓ cup *olive oil* or *salad oil*, 2 tablespoons snipped *fresh basil* or 2 teaspoons crushed *dried basil*, 1 tablespoon snipped *fresh tarragon* or 1 teaspoon crushed *dried tarragon*, 2 tablespoons *white wine vinegar*, 2 teaspoons *lemon juice*, 1 clove *minced garlic*, ⅛ teaspoon *ground red pepper* and dash *salt*. Mix well.

COOKOUT VEGETABLE SALAD

At their Lake Isabel, North Dakota, cottage, Marlene and Duane Bohrer wrangle up a
local cookout favorite: pitchfork fondue (prepared in a huge kettle). Marlene's colorful side
dish is the perfect accompaniment to the whole-steak fondue or your favorite grilled meat.

2   10-ounce packages frozen
    Italian-style green
    beans
¼   cup butter or margarine
6   slices bread, cubed
    (4½ cups)
2   12-ounce cans vacuum-
    packed whole-kernel
    corn, drained
1   cup mayonnaise or salad
    dressing
¼   cup chopped pimiento
2   teaspoons dried basil,
    crushed, or
    2 tablespoons snipped
    fresh basil
1   teaspoon garlic salt

1. Cook beans according to package directions; drain and cool.

2. In large skillet, melt butter; add bread cubes. Cook over medium-low heat for 5 to 7 minutes or till bread cubes are crisp and golden brown; set aside.

3. Stir corn, mayonnaise or salad dressing, pimiento, basil and garlic salt into the beans. Turn into a serving bowl. Top with croutons. (Or, cover and chill salad without the croutons; add croutons just before serving.) Makes 12 servings.

BLUE-CHEESE COLESLAW

If they're cooking out for a big gang, Judie and Bob Weil of St. Louis Park, Minnesota,
double this tangy slaw recipe.

1   medium head red
    cabbage, shredded
    (6 cups)
1   cup snipped fresh parsley
¼   cup crumbled blue
    cheese (1 ounce)
¾   cup mayonnaise or salad
    dressing
¼   cup coarse-grain
    Dijon-style mustard

1. In a large bowl, toss cabbage, parsley and cheese together.

2. Combine mayonnaise and mustard. Add to the cabbage and toss well.

3. Cover and chill slaw for at least 2 hours before serving. Top with additional crumbled blue cheese, if you like. Serves 8 to 10.

FIRST-CROP SALAD

When the first crop of spinach comes up in the Midwest, local chefs combine it with other tender, young greens and vegetables, then toss it with a tangy vinaigrette.

½ cup salad oil
2 tablespoons red wine vinegar
1 tablespoon lemon juice
1 teaspoon snipped fresh dillweed
3 cups torn leaf lettuce
3 cups torn spinach
½ cup sliced mushrooms
½ cup sliced radishes
½ cup sliced green onion

1. In a jar, combine salad oil, vinegar, lemon juice, dillweed, ¼ teaspoon *salt* and dash *pepper*. Cover; chill.

2. At serving time, in a large salad bowl, combine remaining ingredients. Shake dressing; pour about *half* over vegetables. Toss to coat vegetables. Refrigerate remaining dressing for another use. Makes 6 to 8 servings.

Note: You can use ¼ teaspoon dried dillweed instead of the snipped dillweed, if you like.

MISSOURI BOTANICAL GARDENS' THREE-BEAN SALAD

A trio of beans combines with other vegetables for a salad as memorable as this St. Louis attraction. If you have fresh herbs, substitute three times as much fresh for the dried.

1 15-ounce can *each* black beans, great northern beans, and garbanzo beans
1 large tomato, chopped
1 cup chopped sweet red and/or green pepper
⅔ cup chopped red onion
½ cup chopped celery
1 tablespoon dried basil
½ teaspoon dried oregano
2 tablespoons snipped fresh parsley
2 tablespoons olive oil
2 tablespoons lemon juice
¼ teaspoon ground red pepper

1. Rinse and drain the beans. In large bowl, combine beans, tomato, sweet pepper, onion and celery.

2. Crushed the dried basil and oregano. In a small bowl, combine basil, oregano, parsley, olive oil, lemon juice, ground red pepper, ¾ cup *water*, ½ teaspoon *salt* and ½ teaspoon *pepper*. Pour over bean mixture and toss well.

3. Cover and refrigerate for 4 to 24 hours. Toss to serve. Makes 8 to 10 servings.

Note: You can substitute red kidney beans for the black beans, if you like.

OLD-FASHIONED SWEET-SOUR COLESLAW

If you want your slaw foamy like the Brookville Hotel in Brookville, Kansas, serves it, owner Mark Martin suggests you dig in with both hands to froth it up.

1 medium head cabbage,
    shredded (6 cups)
1 teaspoon salt
⅔ cup sugar
⅓ cup cider vinegar
1 cup whipping cream

1. Place cabbage in a bowl. Cover; chill for several hours or overnight.

2. Thirty minutes before serving, combine salt, sugar, vinegar and whipping cream in a small bowl. Chill.

3. Just before serving, mix dressing into the cabbage. Makes about 12 servings.

MIXED GREENS SALAD WITH LEMON-MUSTARD DRESSING

The tang of the lemon and bite of the mustard dress up this festive salad, served at Michigan's Saugatuck/Douglas Old English Feaste.

   Lemon-Mustard
      Dressing
1 10-ounce bag spinach,
    washed and torn
    (8 cups)
1 small head Boston leaf
    lettuce, torn (2½ cups)
1 small Belgian endive
8 ounces mushrooms,
    thinly sliced
2 large tomatoes, cut into
    wedges

1. Prepare Lemon-Mustard Dressing. Cover and chill the dressing till serving time.

2. In a chilled salad bowl, combine spinach and lettuce. Cut endive in half, crosswise. Remove the top leaves. Cut the bottoms into wedges. Add leaves and wedges to the salad bowl with mushrooms and tomatoes.

3. Pour desired amount of dressing over salad and toss to serve. Makes 8 to 10 servings.

LEMON-MUSTARD DRESSING: Grate 1 teaspoon peel from a large *lemon*. Then, juice the lemon to get *3 tablespoons* juice. In a small, screw-top jar, combine lemon peel, juice, ⅔ cup *olive oil*, 2 teaspoons *sugar*, ½ teaspoon *salt*, 1 teaspoon *dry mustard*, 1 teaspoon snipped *fresh chives* and ½ teaspoon *freshly cracked pepper* or regular *pepper*. Cover and shake well. Makes about ¾ cup.

COOL CUCUMBER SURPRISE

When Elvira Beckenhauer of Omaha, Nebraska, entered our gelatin salad contest, she mentioned that she wasn't sure cucumbers really belonged in Jell-O® the day she tried this salad. Now, she's convinced they do—and our judges concurred.

1 3-ounce package lemon-flavored gelatin
2 tablespoons vinegar
1 8-ounce carton dairy sour cream
½ cup mayonnaise or salad dressing
2 cups chopped, seeded cucumber
1 tablespoon finely chopped onion

1. Dissolve gelatin and ¼ teaspoon *salt* in 1 cup *boiling water*. Stir in vinegar. Chill the mixture till partially set.

2. Stir together the sour cream, mayonnaise or salad dressing and dash *pepper*. Fold into gelatin mixture. Fold in cucumber and onion.

3. Pour into 5-cup mold. Cover; chill till firm. Unmold onto a lettuce-lined plate, if you like. Makes 6 to 8 servings.

TROPICAL MADONNA SALAD

Virginia Garrelts of Salina, Kansas, won the prize for the most unusual ingredients—peach schnapps and apricot baby food—with this entry in our gelatin salad contest.

1 8-ounce can crushed pineapple
½ cup frozen orange-juice concentrate, thawed
1 3-ounce package apricot-flavored gelatin
¼ cup sugar
1 8-ounce carton piña colada-flavored yogurt
1 6-ounce jar apricots-with-tapioca baby food
1 tablespoon peach schnapps (optional)
1 envelope whipped dessert topping mix
2 tablespoons chopped nuts

1. Drain pineapple, reserving juice. In a saucepan, combine ¾ cup *water*, juice concentrate and reserved pineapple juice. Bring to boiling. Remove from heat. Stir in gelatin and sugar till dissolved. Cover and set aside ⅓ *cup* gelatin mixture at room temperature.

2. Cool remaining gelatin slightly. Whisk in yogurt, apricot baby food and schnapps, if you like. Chill till partially set. Add pineapple; pour into 2-quart round dish. Chill till set.

3. Prepare topping mix according to package directions. Fold in reserved gelatin mixture. Spread over set gelatin. Chill several hours or overnight. Sprinkle with nuts. Serves 9.

Note: Do not use fresh pineapple.

MELBA MOLD SWIRL

When Shirley Choss of Frankfort, Michigan, makes this salad, she picks raspberries and peaches from her garden near Lake Michigan. This is another favorite pick of our taste panel in our gelatin salad contest.

3 3-ounce packages raspberry-flavored gelatin
3 cups boiling water
2 10-ounce packages frozen raspberries, thawed
2 cups peeled and chopped fresh or drained canned peaches
2 teaspoons grated orange peel
2 8-ounce cartons peach or raspberry yogurt

1. Dissolve gelatin in boiling water.

2. Drain raspberries, reserving juice. Add enough cold water to reserved juice to make 1⅔ cups. Stir into gelatin mixture. Chill till partially set.

3. Fold in berries, peaches and orange peel. Fold in yogurt, making swirls.

4. Turn into 13x9x2-inch baking pan. Cover; chill till set. Cut into squares. Serves 12.

CREAMY WHITE FRUIT SALAD

Peggy Fuchs of Nevis, Minnesota, has served this smooth, creamy salad dozens of times— and every time, the white creation draws oohs and ahs. The judges in our gelatin salad contest agreed that this easy-to-make salad is a winner.

2 packages unflavored gelatin
½ cup sugar
2 cups pineapple juice
3 tablespoons lemon juice
1 teaspoon almond extract
   Dash salt
1 cup half-and-half or light cream
1 cup whipping cream
   Fresh strawberries, grapes, sliced kiwi, sliced bananas and/or fresh raspberries

1. In a medium saucepan, stir together the unflavored gelatin and the sugar. Stir in the pineapple juice, lemon juice, almond extract and salt. Cook and stir the mixture over low heat till the gelatin dissolves. Chill the mixture in the refrigerator for about 1 hour or till cool.

2. Stir in half-and-half. Chill till partially set (the consistency of unbeaten egg whites).

3. In a mixing bowl, beat cream till soft peaks form (tips curl). Fold into gelatin mixture. Pour into a 5- or 6-cup mold. Chill till set.

4. Unmold onto a serving platter and arrange fresh fruit around mold. Serves 6 to 8.

CORN-TOMATO SCALLOP

This old-time dish is part of the 1900s dinner at Des Moines' Living History Farms.

2   14½- or 16-ounce cans
    whole tomatoes
1   8¾-ounce can
    cream-style corn
1   8-ounce can whole-
    kernel corn, drained
2   slightly beaten eggs
2   tablespoons all-purpose
    flour
2   teaspoons sugar
¼   cup butter or margarine
1   medium onion, finely
    chopped
1   clove garlic, minced
4   cups soft bread crumbs
½   cup grated Parmesan
    cheese (2 ounces)

1. Drain and cut up the tomatoes. Combine tomatoes, cream-style corn, drained whole-kernel corn, eggs, flour, sugar and ½ teaspoon *pepper*. Turn corn mixture into a 2-quart rectangular baking dish.

2. In a medium saucepan, melt butter or margarine. Add the onion and garlic. Cook till onion is tender, but not brown.

3. Combine bread crumbs and Parmesan cheese. Add the butter mixture to the bread-crumb mixture and toss to combine. Sprinkle over the baking dish.

4. Bake in a 350° oven for about 30 minutes or till a knife inserted near the center comes out clean. Makes 8 servings.

GLORIA'S SAVORY BEANS

Gloria Sextro of St. Louis, Missouri, tosses lima beans, green beans and red onion with an herbed olive-oil dressing blend for this mild side dish she serves at barbecues.

1   10-ounce package frozen
    lima beans
1   9-ounce package frozen
    French-style green
    beans
3   shallots or green onions,
    chopped
1   clove garlic, minced
2   tablespoons olive oil or
    cooking oil
1   teaspoon dried savory
1   small red onion, thinly
    sliced
    Salt and pepper

1. In a large saucepan, bring ¾ cup *water* to boiling. Add lima beans. Return to boiling and cook for 5 minutes. Add green beans. Cook for 3 minutes more or till the beans are crisp-tender. Drain.

2. Meanwhile, in a medium skillet, cook shallots and garlic in hot oil for 2 minutes. Crush savory; add to skillet and cook for 2 minutes more. Stir in red onion, ¼ teaspoon *salt* and ⅛ teaspoon *pepper*. Cook for 2 minutes more.

3. In a serving bowl, toss together beans and red onion mixture. Season with *salt* and *pepper*. Makes 6 servings.

CALICO BEANS

In minutes, Kathy Mountain of St. Marys, Iowa, has this savory bean trio ready to simmer in her crockery cooker.

¼ **pound bacon (5 slices)**
1 **medium onion, chopped**
1 **28- or 31-ounce can pork and beans with tomato sauce or one 27½-ounce can pork and beans with brown sugar**
1 **15-ounce can butter beans, drained**
1 **15-ounce can pinto beans, drained**
½ **cup packed brown sugar**
½ **cup ketchup**
2 **tablespoons vinegar**
1 **teaspoon dry mustard**
1 **teaspoon salt**

1. In a skillet, cook bacon till crisp. Drain bacon, reserving 2 tablespoons drippings; crumble bacon. Cook onion in drippings till tender, but not brown.

2. In a 3½- or 4-quart crockery cooker, combine bacon, onion and remaining ingredients; mix well. Cover. Cook bean mixture on low-heat setting for 4½ to 5½ hours. Uncover and cook on high-heat setting for 30 minutes more. (Or, cook on high-heat setting for the entire cooking time, 3 to 3½ hours, uncovering for the last 30 minutes.) Serves 10 to 12.

To Oven Bake
Prepare bacon and onion as above. Transfer to a 2-quart round casserole with remaining ingredients; mix well. Bake, uncovered, in a 350° oven for 1¼ to 1½ hours. Stir.

HOMINY GRITS BAKE

Marilyn Schudy of Kansas City, Missouri, inherited this recipe from her mother.

4 **cups water**
1 **cup quick-cooking hominy grits**
1 **teaspoon seasoned salt**
1½ **cups shredded sharp cheddar cheese (6 ounces)**
¼ **cup butter or margarine**
Several dashes Worcestershire sauce
3 **well-beaten eggs**

1. In large saucepan, bring water to boiling. Slowly add grits and seasoned salt, stirring constantly. Cook and stir till boiling. Reduce heat; cook and stir for 5 to 6 minutes more or till all water is absorbed and mixture is thick.

2. Add shredded cheese, margarine and Worcestershire; stir till cheese and butter are melted. Gradually stir into beaten eggs.

3. Turn into a greased 1½-quart round casserole or 2-quart soufflé dish. Bake, uncovered, in a 350° oven for about 1 hour or till nearly set. Let stand for 10 minutes. Serves 8 to 10.

CARROTS IN ORANGE GLAZE

Honey and brown sugar make a shiny glaze for bias-sliced carrots in this dish, featured at a black-tie fundraiser for the Des Moines Symphony Orchestra.

2 tablespoons butter or margarine
2 tablespoons brown sugar
2 tablespoons honey
2 teaspoons finely shredded orange peel
Dash salt
Dash pepper
6 medium carrots, thinly bias sliced (about 3 cups, 1 pound)

1. In a medium saucepan, melt butter or margarine. Stir in brown sugar, honey, orange peel, salt and pepper.

2. Add the carrots and cook, uncovered, over medium heat for 8 to 10 minutes or till carrots are just crisp-tender, stirring mixture occasionally. Makes 4 servings.

SAVORY BABY CARROTS

Marilyn Hampstead grows mini vegetables at her Fox Hill Farm in Parma, Michigan. She tosses some of her baby carrots and turnips with honey and cheese for this tasty dish.

1 pound baby carrots, tops trimmed to 1½ inches
¼ pound baby turnips with fine greens or 1 medium turnip cut into 6 wedges
1 tablespoon olive or cooking oil
2 tablespoons snipped fresh sage or rosemary, or 2 teaspoons dried sage or rosemary, crushed
1 clove garlic, minced
2 tablespoons honey
¼ cup grated Parmesan or Romano cheese (1 ounce)

1. Cook carrots and turnips in boiling salted water for 4 minutes. Drain.

2. In skillet, heat oil over medium-high heat. Add herb and garlic. Stir-fry for 10 seconds. Add vegetables. Stir-fry till lightly browned and crisp-tender, for about 5 minutes. Season with *salt* and *pepper*.

3. Toss with honey and Parmesan or Romano cheese. Makes 6 servings.

CHEESY BROCCOLI BAKE

For family Christmas dinners in North Dakota, Jane Sinner, wife of former Governor George Sinner, dresses up this vegetable dish for the season.

¼ cup chopped onion
2 tablespoons butter
2 tablespoons all-purpose flour
½ cup water or milk
1 8-ounce jar cheese spread or one 8-ounce package cheese spread, cubed
3 10-ounce packages frozen chopped broccoli, cooked and drained
3 beaten eggs
⅓ cup crushed cornflakes

1. In 3-quart saucepan, cook onion in butter till tender but not brown. Stir in flour. Add water. Cook and stir till thick and bubbly. Blend in cheese spread. Remove from heat. Stir in broccoli, then eggs. Transfer to a 1½-quart round casserole. Top with cornflakes.

2. Bake casserole, uncovered, in a 325° oven for about 50 minutes or till knife inserted halfway between edge and center comes out clean. Let stand for 10 minutes before serving. Makes 8 servings.

To Use Your Microwave
Prepare as above, reserving cornflakes and using a microwave-safe casserole. Cover. Microcook on 70% power (medium high) for 10 to 12 minutes or till set, giving casserole a half turn every 5 minutes. Sprinkle with cornflakes. Let stand for 10 minutes.

CREAMED-STYLE CORN

A simple sauce adds to the corn flavor in this dish from Mark and Connie Martin, owners of the Brookville Hotel in Brookville, Kansas. Try it with fresh-off-the-cob sweet corn, too.

2 10-ounce packages frozen whole-kernel corn
¼ cup whipping cream or light cream
1½ teaspoons sugar
½ teaspoon salt
1½ teaspoons cornstarch
2 tablespoons whipping cream or light cream

1. In a 2-quart saucepan, cook corn according to package directions. Drain. Add the ¼ cup cream, sugar and salt. Bring just to boiling.

2. Meanwhile, combine the cornstarch and the 2 tablespoons cream. Stir into the corn mixture. Cook and stir till thickened and bubbly; cook 2 minutes more. Makes about 6 servings.

BRAISED RED CABBAGE

This subtly spiced sweet-sour dish comes from German-American chef Erwin Pfeil of the Golden Lamb in Lebanon, Ohio.

1 medium head red
   cabbage (about
   2 pounds)
½ cup dry red wine
2 tablespoons vinegar
2 tablespoons lemon juice
1 tablespoon sugar
1 teaspoon salt
¼ teaspoon pepper
1 bay leaf
3 whole cloves
2 whole allspice
½ cup chopped onion
1 tablespoon butter or
   margarine
½ cup water
2 tablespoons currant jelly
   Apple slices (optional)
   Lemon juice (optional)

1. Cut cabbage into quarters; core. Using a sharp knife, cut cabbage into julienne slices or shred into finer pieces. Transfer cabbage to a large mixing bowl.

2. Stir together wine, vinegar, the 2 table-spoons lemon juice, sugar, salt and pepper. Pour over cabbage; toss to coat. Tie bay leaf, cloves and allspice in cheesecloth bag. Push under surface of cabbage mixture. Cover; store in refrigerator overnight.

3. In a large saucepan, cook onion in butter or margarine till tender but not brown. Add *undrained* cabbage mixture, water and currant jelly. Bring to boiling. Reduce heat; simmer, covered, for 15 minutes for crisp cabbage, about 30 minutes for tender cabbage. Remove spice bag; transfer to serving dish.

4. If you like, dip the apple slices in lemon juice; garnish the cabbage with the apple slices. Makes 6 to 8 servings.

SPUDS À LA ELEGANT

This cheesy casserole from North Dakota is pretty, fluffy and flavorsome.

6   medium potatoes
    (2 pounds), peeled
    and quartered
1   8-ounce package cream
    cheese, softened
1   beaten egg
¼   teaspoon salt
⅓   cup finely chopped onion
¼   cup diced pimiento

1. Cook potatoes in boiling, lightly salted water for 20 to 25 minutes or till tender; drain. Mash potatoes. Add cream cheese, egg, salt and dash *pepper*; beat till smooth. Stir in onion and pimiento. If mixture seems dry, stir in 1 to 2 tablespoons *milk*.

2. Transfer to buttered 1-quart round casserole. Bake, covered, in 325° oven 40 to 45 minutes. Makes 6 to 8 servings.

FRUITED SWEET POTATOES

This reminder of bygone holiday feasts comes from the Apple Haus in Long Grove, Illinois. It's updated with apples and a crunchy topping.

6   medium sweet potatoes
    (about 2 pounds)
2   medium apples, peeled
    and thinly sliced
¼   cup chopped pecans
1   tablespoon butter or
    margarine
½   cup orange juice
2   tablespoons brown sugar
½   teaspoon ground
    cinnamon
3   tablespoons fine dry
    bread crumbs
2   tablespoons brown sugar
1   tablespoon butter or
    margarine, softened
12 large marshmallows

1. In a large saucepan, cook sweet potatoes in enough boiling water to cover for 20 to 25 minutes or till tender. Drain, cool and peel sweet potatoes. Cut into ¼-inch-thick slices. Place in a buttered 2-quart rectangular baking dish along with apples. Sprinkle with pecans.

2. In saucepan, melt the 1 tablespoon butter. Add juice, 2 tablespoons brown sugar and cinnamon. Bring to boiling. Pour orange-juice mixture over sweet potatoes and apples. Bake, covered with foil, in a 350° oven for 25 to 30 minutes or till apples are tender.

3. Combine bread crumbs, remaining 2 tablespoons brown sugar and 1 tablespoon softened butter to make a crumbly mixture. Uncover casserole; sprinkle with crumb mixture. Arrange marshmallows over mixture. Bake, uncovered, for 10 minutes more or till the marshmallows are golden. Makes 6 servings.

WISCONSIN POTATO PATTIES

According to innkeeper Bertha Mueller, guests at The Wisconsin House Stagecoach Inn in Hazel Green, Wisconsin, often say, " Oh, I haven't had these in a long time."

4 cups cold mashed
    potatoes
½ cup light cream or milk
12 soda crackers, crushed
    (about ½ cup crumbs)
1 small onion, finely
    chopped (¼ cup)
1 slightly beaten egg
¼ teaspoon celery salt
¼ teaspoon pepper
⅛ teaspoon garlic salt

1. In a mixing bowl, combine potatoes, cream or milk, cracker crumbs, onion, egg, celery salt, pepper and garlic salt. Shape the potato mixture into twelve ½-inch-thick patties.

2. Cook on a greased, preheated griddle over medium heat or in an electric skillet at 350° for 3 to 4 minutes or till brown and warm on top. Turn and cook for 3 to 4 minutes more or till brown. (For crispier potato patties, fry in more shortening or cooking oil.) Keep warm in a 300° oven while cooking remaining patties. Makes 12 patties.

SWABIAN POTATO DUMPLINGS

According to German-American chef Erwin Pfeil of the Golden Lamb in Lebanon, Ohio, the secret to successful dumplings: Don't lift the lid while they're cooking.

3 medium potatoes, peeled
    and quartered
2 slices bacon
½ cup chopped onion
1 tablespoon butter or
    margarine
1 cup ¼- to ⅜-inch cubes
    French bread
2 tablespoons snipped
    fresh parsley
3 beaten eggs
½ cup all-purpose flour
1 teaspoon salt
    Dash ground nutmeg
    Dash white pepper

1. In a large saucepan, cook potatoes in boiling, lightly salted water for 20 to 25 minutes or till tender. Drain and mash. Meanwhile, cook bacon till crisp; drain and crumble. Fill a deep 12-inch skillet half full with water; bring water to boiling.

2. In a saucepan, cook onion in butter or margarine till tender but not brown. Stir in bread cubes, crumbled bacon and parsley. Stir the onion mixture into the mashed potatoes.

3. In a bowl, combine eggs, flour, salt, nutmeg and white pepper. Add to potato mixture. With floured hands, shape into 2½-inch balls. Drop dumplings into the boiling water. Return to boiling; cover tightly. Reduce heat; *do not lift cover*. Cook dumplings for 15 minutes or till done. Makes 8 servings.

PASTA WITH PORCHINI MUSHROOM SAUCE

Rina Fontanini of Highland Park, Illinois, cooks big batches of this Italian sauce to serve over her homemade pasta.

½ cup dried porchini mushrooms or other dried mushrooms
1 medium onion, chopped
2 large cloves garlic, minced
2 tablespoons butter or margarine
2 tablespoons olive oil or cooking oil
1 cup whipping cream
1 6-ounce can tomato paste
1 teaspoon instant chicken bouillon granules
1 teaspoon dried marjoram, crushed
½ teaspoon salt
¼ teaspoon pepper
6 to 8 ounces fresh or dried tagliatelle or fettuccine

1. Rehydrate mushrooms according to package directions; drain off liquid. Cut up any large mushrooms.

2. Cook mushrooms, onion and garlic in hot butter and olive oil till tender.

3. Stir in cream, tomato paste, bouillon, marjoram, salt and pepper. Heat through.

4. Meanwhile, cook the tagliatelle or fettuccine in boiling, salted water till just tender; drain. Serve the warm pasta topped with mushroom sauce. Makes 6 side-dish servings.

BREADS

*Kansas
Honey-Wheat
Sunflower
Bread*

BREADS

KANSAS HONEY-WHEAT SUNFLOWER BREAD

This hearty whole-wheat-and-honey bread is chock-full of crunchy nuts—the precious bounty of the Kansas state flower, the sunflower. Try a thick slice warm from the oven. It's like eating honey cake.

2 cups lukewarm water (120° to 130°)
2¾ to 3¼ cups bread or all-purpose flour
2 packages active dry yeast
1 tablespoon sugar
2 cups whole-wheat flour
1 cup rolled oats
⅓ cup instant non-fat dry milk
¼ cup butter or margarine, softened
¼ cup honey
2 teaspoons salt
1 cup unsalted sunflower nuts

1. In a large mixing bowl, combine the water, *2 cups* of the bread or all-purpose flour, yeast and sugar. Beat with electric mixer on low speed for 3 minutes. Cover and let dough rise till double (30 minutes). The mixture will become spongy.

2. Stir in whole-wheat flour, oats, dry milk, butter or margarine, honey and salt. Mix well. Stir in sunflower nuts, then mix in as much of the remaining bread or all-purpose flour as you can with a spoon.

3. Turn out onto a floured surface and knead in enough remaining flour to make a moderately stiff dough (6 to 8 minutes). Shape into a ball. Place in a greased bowl; turn once. Cover and let rise in a warm place till double (30 to 45 minutes).

4. Punch dough down. Turn out onto a lightly floured surface. Divide in half. Cover; let rest for 10 minutes. Shape into loaves. Place in 2 greased 8x4x2-inch loaf pans.

5. Cover; let rise in a warm place till almost double (30 minutes).

6. Bake loaves in a 375° oven for about 35 minutes, covering with foil the last 15 minutes to prevent overbrowning. Remove from pans and cool on wire racks. Makes 2 loaves.

MOLASSES WHOLE-WHEAT BRAID

This hearty, five-grain braided loaf is served at the Elizabethan Christmas Feaste that
Saugatuck and Douglas innkeepers host in Douglas, Michigan.

3½ to 4 cups whole-wheat flour
2 cups rye flour
1 cup unprocessed wheat bran
½ cup wheat germ
2 packages active dry yeast
3 tablespoons sugar
1 teaspoon salt
1 cup water
¾ cup milk
½ cup butter or margarine
⅓ cup dark molasses
1 egg
1 egg yolk
2 tablespoons cornmeal
1 egg white
1 tablespoon water
1 teaspoon caraway seed

1. Combine *3 cups* of the whole-wheat flour, rye flour, bran and wheat germ. In a mixing bowl, combine 3 cups of flour mixture, yeast, sugar and salt. Heat together 1 cup water, milk, butter and molasses till very warm (120° to 130°) and butter is almost melted. With electric mixer on low speed, gradually beat warm liquid into yeast mixture. Beat 2 minutes on medium speed, scraping bowl often.

2. Beat egg, yolk and 1 cup of the flour mixture into yeast dough; beat 2 minutes more. Using a spoon, stir in remaining flour mixture. Turn out onto a surface floured with some of the whole-wheat flour. Knead in enough of the remaining whole-wheat flour till dough is smooth and elastic (6 to 8 minutes).

3. Shape into ball. Place in greased bowl, turning once. Cover; let rise in a warm place till double (about 1 hour). Punch down. Turn out onto floured surface. Divide into 3 portions. Cover; let rest 10 minutes.

4. Sprinkle a lightly greased baking sheet with cornmeal. Shape dough into three 24-inch-long ropes. Place ropes 1 inch apart on baking sheet. Starting at center, loosely braid ropes; tuck under ends. Cover and let rise till almost double (about 30 minutes).

5. Mix egg white and 1 tablespoon water; brush over bread. Sprinkle with caraway seed. Bake in a 350° oven for about 45 minutes or till done, covering with foil the last 10 minutes. Remove to rack to cool. Makes 1 loaf.

LUCK O' THE IRISH WHOLE-WHEAT BREAD

Jim Navin of Oconomowoc, Wisconsin, has been baking breads for years, but "official" recognition came when his yeast bread won first place at the Milwaukee Irish Fest. Jim's recipe makes four loaves (we only had one bowl in our Test Kitchen that would hold all the dough, so we halved the original recipe).

2   cakes compressed yeast or 2 packages active dry yeast

2   cups warm water (85° for compressed or 110° for active dry)

¼   cup butter or margarine, melted

1   tablespoon salt

3½   cups whole-wheat flour

⅓   cup honey

3   to 3½ cups unbleached flour or all-purpose flour

1. In a large mixing bowl, combine yeast and water. Stir to dissolve yeast. Stir in the melted butter and salt.

2. Add the whole-wheat flour and mix well. Let stand for 3 to 5 minutes. Stir in the honey.

3. Stir in as much unbleached flour as you can. Turn out onto a floured surface; knead in enough remaining flour to make a stiff dough that's smooth and elastic (8 to 10 minutes).

4. Place the dough in a greased bowl. Cover; let rise till double in size (1¼ hours). Punch down; let rise again till almost double (about 45 minutes).

5. Divide dough; shape and place in two greased 8x4x2- or 9x5x3-inch loaf pans. Cover; let rise till nearly double and center is rounded (45 minutes).

6. Bake in a 350° oven for 45 to 50 minutes or till done. Cover with foil after 30 minutes, if necessary, to prevent overbrowning. Remove from pans and cool on wire racks. Brush the tops with additional *melted butter* while warm, if you like. Makes 2 loaves.

QUICK RYE-BATTER BUNS

These buns are a tasty alternative to the usual rye bread, which is typical fish-boil fare in Wisconsin's Door County. Sprinkle the buns with caraway seed before baking, if you like.

3 cups all-purpose flour
2 packages quick-rising active dry yeast
2 cups milk
½ cup packed dark brown sugar
3 tablespoons cooking oil
1½ teaspoons salt
2 eggs
1 teaspoon caraway seed (optional)
2 cups rye flour
Milk

1. In a large mixing bowl, combine the all-purpose flour and yeast. In a saucepan, heat the 2 cups milk, dark brown sugar, cooking oil and salt till warm (120° to 130°), stirring constantly. Add to the flour mixture. Add the eggs and the caraway seed, if you like.

2. Beat the batter with electric mixer on low speed for 30 seconds, scraping sides of bowl. Beat the batter on high speed for 3 minutes. Return to low speed and beat in rye flour.

3. Fill greased muffin pans half full. Cover and let the dough rise till double, about 25 minutes. Bake in a 400° oven for 10 minutes. Brush the buns with milk. Bake for 5 to 10 minutes more or till done. Remove the buns from the pans; cool. Makes about 24.

ORANGE FILLING AND GLAZE

Use this citrusy filling and glaze for the Wheat Cinnamon Rolls on page 81.

¾ cup sugar
½ cup softened butter
4 teaspoons ground cinnamon
1 tablespoon finely shredded orange peel
2 teaspoons all-purpose flour
4 cups sifted powdered sugar
1 teaspoon vanilla
4 to 6 tablespoons orange juice

1. To prepare Orange Filling, combine sugar, butter, cinnamon, peel and flour.

2. To prepare Orange Glaze, combine powdered sugar and vanilla. Add enough of the orange juice to make drizzling consistency.

WHEAT CINNAMON ROLLS

Our editors developed these yummy, two-fisted sweet rolls—a Heartland favorite.

4½ to 5 cups all-purpose
     flour
 2 packages active dry yeast
1½ cups milk
 ½ cup butter or margarine
 ½ cup sugar
 1 teaspoon salt
 3 eggs
 2 cups whole-wheat flour
     Orange Filling (see
        recipe, page 80)
 1 cup chopped nuts
     Orange Glaze (see recipe,
        page 80)

1. In a large mixing bowl, combine *3 cups* of the all-purpose flour and the yeast. Heat and stir milk, butter, sugar and salt till just warm (120° to 130°) and butter is almost melted.

2. Add to flour mixture. Add eggs and beat with an electric mixer on low speed for 30 seconds, scraping bowl constantly. Using a spoon, stir in whole-wheat flour and as much of the remaining all-purpose flour as you can.

3. Turn dough out onto a lightly floured surface. Knead in enough of the remaining flour to make a moderately stiff dough that's smooth and elastic (6 to 8 minutes total). Shape into a ball. Place in a greased bowl, turning once. Cover and let rise in a warm place till double (about 1 hour).

4. Punch dough down. Divide in half. Cover and let rest for 10 minutes. On a lightly floured surface, roll each half of dough into a 12-inch square. Spread half of the Orange Filling over each. Sprinkle each with half of the chopped nuts. Roll up each square, jelly-roll style. Seal edges. Slice each roll of dough into 8 pieces. Place the pieces in a greased 13x9x2-inch baking pan. Repeat with remaining pieces, using another greased 13x9x2-inch pan or a 12-inch pizza pan.

5. Cover and let rise in a warm place for about 45 minutes or till nearly double.

6. Uncover; bake in 375° oven for 10 minutes. Cover loosely with foil; bake 10 to 15 minutes. Cool slightly. Drizzle with Orange Glaze. Makes 16 rolls.

CINNAMON BREAD

This Midwest bread classic is especially delicious toasted.

6¾ to 7¼ cups all-purpose flour
2 packages active dry yeast
1 cup milk
¾ cup water
⅓ cup sugar
⅓ cup margarine or butter
1½ teaspoons salt
3 eggs
¼ cup butter or margarine, softened
½ cup sugar
4 teaspoons ground cinnamon
1 slightly beaten egg white

1. In a large mixing bowl, combine *3 cups* of the flour and yeast. In a 1-quart saucepan, heat milk, water, ⅓ cup sugar, ⅓ cup butter and salt just till warm (115° to 120°) and margarine is almost melted, stirring constantly.

2. Add liquid mixture to flour mixture. Add eggs. Beat on low speed with an electric mixer for 30 seconds, scraping sides of bowl. Beat on high speed 3 minutes. Using a spoon, mix in as much of remaining flour as you can.

3. On a lightly floured surface, knead in enough of remaining flour to make moderately stiff dough that is smooth and elastic (6 to 8 minutes total). Shape into ball. Place in lightly greased bowl; turn once to grease surface. Cover; let rise in a warm place till double (about 1¼ hours).

4. Punch dough down. Cover; let rest 10 minutes. Divide in half. Roll each half into 14x9-inch rectangle. Brush entire surface of each rectangle with half of the softened margarine.

5. Combine ½ cup sugar and cinnamon; sprinkle half over each rectangle. Beginning with the narrow side, roll up jelly-roll style; seal edge and ends. Place, sealed edges down, in two greased 9x5x3-inch loaf pans. Cover; let rise till nearly double (30 to 45 minutes).

6. Brush dough with egg white. Bake, uncovered, in a 375° oven for 35 to 40 minutes or till done, covering with foil after 20 minutes of baking to prevent overbrowning. Remove from pans. Cool on racks. Makes 2 loaves.

BABKA

A family brunch is an Easter tradition at the Frank and Marilyn Schudy home in Kansas City, Missouri. Frank's grandmother contributed the recipe for this Polish sweet bread.

4 to 4½ cups unbleached or all-purpose flour
1 package active dry yeast
½ cup butter or margarine
¼ cup warm water
⅔ cup sugar
½ cup light cream or milk
½ teaspoon salt
½ teaspoon vanilla
5 egg yolks
2 eggs
1 cup light raisins
Confectioner's Icing

1. In a large mixing bowl, combine *2 cups* of the flour and the yeast. Heat butter, warm water, sugar, cream and salt till warm (115° to 120°) and margarine is almost melted, stirring constantly. Stir in vanilla.

2. Add liquid mixture to flour mixture. Add yolks and eggs. Beat on low speed for ½ minute, scraping bowl. Beat on high speed for 3 minutes. Using spoon, mix in as much of the remaining flour as you can. Stir in raisins.

3. On a lightly floured surface, knead in enough of the remaining flour to make moderately soft dough that is smooth and elastic (3 to 5 minutes total). Shape into ball. Place in lightly greased bowl; turn once. Cover; let rise in warm place till double (about 1½ hours).

4. Punch dough down. Cover; let rest 10 minutes. Grease 10-cup kugelhopf mold or 12-cup fluted tube pan; coat lightly with *flour*. Shape dough into rope about 15 inches long and 3 inches wide. Press evenly and firmly into pan, curving it around the center tube. Cover; let rise till nearly double (about 1 hour).

5. Bake, uncovered, in a 350° oven 40 minutes or till done, covering with foil during last 10 minutes. Remove from pan. Cool completely on a wire rack. Drizzle with Confectioner's Icing. Makes 1 loaf.

CONFECTIONER'S ICING: Mix 2 cups sifted *powdered sugar*, 1 teaspoon *lemon juice* and 1 teaspoon *vanilla*. Stir in enough *milk* for drizzling consistency (2 to 4 tablespoons).

BOUSKA KOLACHE

Czechs prepare kolache with different fillings, including poppy seed, prune and peach. Frances Bouska makes her kolache for occasions such as weddings and Tabor Czech Days. They're held every June in Tabor, South Dakota.

1¼ cups warm milk (80° to 90° for compressed yeast, 105° to 115° for dry yeast)
1 cake compressed yeast, crumbled, or
    1 package active dry yeast
½ teaspoon sugar
1 egg
1 egg yolk
¼ cup sugar
6 tablespoons cooking oil
¼ cup whipping cream
3½ to 4 cups all-purpose flour
½ teaspoon salt
    Peach Filling
    Coconut-Streusel Topping (optional)
3 tablespoons water
1 tablespoon sugar

1. Combine ⅓ cup of the milk, yeast and ½ teaspoon sugar; let stand at room temperature till foamy. Beat egg and yolk; stir in ¼ cup sugar, oil, cream and remaining milk.

2. Stir together 1 cup of the flour and salt. Add yeast and egg mixtures; beat smooth. Beat in enough remaining flour, ¼ cup at a time, to make a soft dough that's slightly sticky. Knead 5 minutes. Cover dough; let rise 1 hour.

3. Shape dough into 1½-inch balls. Place on a greased baking pan, 3 inches apart. Let rise till double, 45 minutes.

4. Make an indentation in each ball, leaving about a ½-inch rim of dough around edge. Spoon in a rounded teaspoon of Peach Filling. Let rise 15 to 20 minutes. Sprinkle with Coconut-Streusel Topping, if you like.

5. Bake in 425° oven 8 minutes. Remove; cool. Heat water and 1 tablespoon sugar till sugar dissolves; brush over pastries. Makes 42.

PEACH FILLING: Cook 1 pound *dried peaches* in 1½ cups *water*, covered, 10 minutes. Blend to puree. Stir in ¾ cup *sugar*, then ½ teaspoon *vanilla* and several dashes *ground cinnamon*. Makes 2½ cups. Freeze extra filling. (Frances says canned pie filling works, too.)

COCONUT-STREUSEL TOPPING: In a blender, finely shred ½ cup *coconut*. Combine with ¾ cup *all-purpose flour* and ¼ cup *sugar*. Cut in ¼ cup *butter*.

PUMPKIN CINNAMON ROLLS

You'll find these cinnamon-spiced, no-knead yeast rolls for sale at roadside tables in Amish country. Caramel icing makes the rolls gooey delicious.

⅓ cup milk
2 tablespoons butter
½ cup canned pumpkin or mashed, cooked pumpkin
2 tablespoons sugar
½ teaspoon salt
1 beaten egg
1 package active dry yeast
1 cup unbleached flour
1 cup bread flour
2 tablespoons butter, melted
⅓ cup packed brown sugar
1 teaspoon ground cinnamon
Caramel Frosting (see recipe, page 86)

1. Heat and stir milk and 2 tablespoons butter till just warm (120° to 130°). In bowl, mix pumpkin, sugar and salt. Add milk mixture; beat with electric mixer till well mixed. Beat in egg and yeast.

2. Combine unbleached flour and bread flour. Add half of flour mixture to the pumpkin mixture. Beat mixture on low speed for 5 minutes, scraping sides of bowl constantly. Add remaining flour; mix thoroughly (dough will be very soft). Turn into a lightly greased bowl; grease surface of dough lightly. Cover and let rise in a warm place till double (about 1 hour).

3. Punch dough down. Turn onto floured surface. Knead a few turns till smooth, sprinkling with enough additional *flour* to make dough easy to handle. On lightly floured surface, roll into a 12x10-inch rectangle.

4. Brush dough with melted butter. Mix brown sugar and cinnamon; sprinkle over dough. Beginning with longest side, roll dough up jelly-roll style; seal seam. With a sharp knife, cut into twelve 1-inch slices. Place rolls, cut side up, in greased 9x9x2-inch baking pan. Cover; let rise till nearly double, 30 to 45 minutes. Bake the shaped rolls in a 350° oven for about 20 minutes or till done.

5. Meanwhile, prepare Caramel Frosting.

6. When rolls are done, immediately remove them from pan to a waxed-paper-lined wire rack. Cool 10 to 15 minutes. Drizzle with Caramel Frosting. Makes 12 rolls.

GLORIA'S JALAPEÑO CORNBREAD

Gloria Sextro of St. Louis always uses peppy jalapeño peppers in this cornbread. For a milder version, try chopped green pepper instead of the jalapeño.

2½ cups yellow cornmeal
½ cup all-purpose flour
2 teaspoons sugar
2 teaspoons baking powder
2 cups milk
1½ cups shredded cheddar cheese (6 ounces)
1 8¾-ounce can cream-style corn
5 slices bacon, crisp-cooked and crumbled
½ cup bacon drippings or cooking oil
½ cup seeded and finely chopped jalapeño peppers
½ cup finely chopped onion
3 slightly beaten eggs
¼ cup drained, chopped pimiento
1 clove garlic, minced

1. In a large mixing bowl, stir together the cornmeal, flour, sugar, baking powder and ½ teaspoon *salt*.

2. In another bowl, combine the remaining ingredients. Add to the cornmeal mixture; stir till just combined.

3. Pour into a greased 13x9x2-inch baking pan. Bake in a 425° oven for about 35 minutes or till brown. Serve warm. Makes 15 servings.

Note: For corn muffins, spoon batter into the greased cups of muffin pans (⅔ full). *Don't use paper bake cups.* Bake in a 425° oven for about 15 minutes or till done. Makes 30.

CARAMEL FROSTING

Make this buttery frosting for the Pumpkin Cinnamon Rolls on page 85.

¼ cup butter
½ cup packed brown sugar
2 tablespoons milk
¼ teaspoon vanilla
Dash salt
¾ cup sifted powdered sugar

1. In a small saucepan heat butter till melted. Stir in brown sugar and milk. Cook over medium-low heat for 1 minute. Transfer to a small mixing bowl; cool.

2. Add vanilla, salt and powdered sugar. Beat with electric mixer till well blended. If necessary, add more powdered sugar to the frosting for desired consistency.

HEAVENLY BELGIAN WAFFLES

Belgian waffles are a mainstay at Midwest brunches. Here's our delicious version, topped with ice cream and a warm fruit-and-pecan sauce.

1¾ cups all-purpose flour
1 tablespoon baking powder
2 tablespoons malted-milk powder
2 egg yolks
1¾ cups milk
½ cup cooking oil or melted shortening
2 egg whites
Vanilla ice cream
Fruit-Pecan Sauce

1. In a large mixing bowl, stir together the flour, baking powder and malted-milk powder.

2. In a medium mixing bowl, beat egg yolks. Beat in the milk and cooking oil or shortening. Add to the flour mixture all at once, stirring till blended but still slightly lumpy.

3. In a small mixing bowl, beat egg whites till stiff peaks form (tips stand straight). Gently fold into the egg-flour mixture, leaving a few fluffs of egg whites. Do not overmix.

4. Bake waffles in Belgian waffle-maker or regular waffle-maker according to manufacturer's directions. (To keep waffles hot for serving, place in a single layer on a wire rack on a baking sheet in a warm oven.)

5. Serve waffles with ice cream and warm Fruit-Pecan Sauce. Makes four 8-inch waffles.

FRUIT-PECAN SAUCE: Peel 4 small ripe *bananas;* cut in half lengthwise, then cut crosswise into thirds. Brush with *lemon juice.* Halve 1 pint *fresh strawberries* or thawed, *frozen, unsweetened strawberries.* In a large skillet, heat ⅔ cup packed *brown sugar* and ⅓ cup *butter* or *margarine* over medium heat till the mixture melts, stirring occasionally.

Add bananas and strawberries; cook, uncovered, till bananas are heated through, turning once. Stir in 2 tablespoons *rum* or *orange juice,* then ½ cup broken, toasted *pecans.*

HOOSIER APPLE-YOGURT COFFEE CAKE

Judges picked this moist oatmeal coffee cake as the winner in the children's category at the New Albany, Indiana, Harvest Baking Contest. Serve the nut-topped specialty warm for breakfast or as a snack.

⅔ cup sugar
½ cup butter or margarine
2 eggs
1 teaspoon vanilla
1¼ cups ground rolled oats (start with 1⅔ cups oats and grind in blender or food processor)
1 cup all-purpose flour
1 teaspoon baking powder
1 teaspoon baking soda
1 8-ounce carton plain yogurt
2 cups finely chopped, peeled cooking apples
½ cup chopped nuts
½ cup packed brown sugar
1 tablespoon butter or margarine, melted

1. In a large mixing bowl, beat together the sugar and butter or margarine till fluffy. Add the eggs and vanilla. Beat well.

2. Combine oats, flour, baking powder and baking soda. Add to beaten mixture alternately with yogurt, beating after each addition till the mixture is just combined.

3. Fold in the apples. Divide batter between two greased and floured 8x1½-inch round baking pans.

4. Mix the nuts, brown sugar and melted butter or margarine. Sprinkle over batter in pans.

5. Bake in a 350° oven for 30 to 35 minutes or till done. Cool coffee cakes in pans on wire racks. Serve warm or cooled. Makes 2 coffee cakes, 6 to 8 servings each.

CARROT BREAD

This dark, easy-to-make, cakelike bread stays moist for days—if it lasts that long. In Iowa, Amish mothers and daughters make it with carrots they grow in their gardens.

2½ cups shredded carrot
1 cup finely chopped pecans
2 cups unbleached flour
1½ cups sugar
2 teaspoons baking powder
2 teaspoons ground cinnamon
1 teaspoon salt
3 eggs
1½ cups cooking oil
2 teaspoons vanilla

1. In a medium bowl, toss together the carrot and pecans; set aside. In another bowl, stir together flour, sugar, baking powder, cinnamon and salt; set aside.

2. In a large mixing bowl, beat eggs with electric mixer. Beat in oil and vanilla. Gradually beat in flour mixture, then carrot mixture. Turn into a well-greased 10-inch tube pan. (Don't bake in a loaf pan; batter in center will not get done before rest of bread is overdone.)

3. Bake in a 325° oven about 1 hour and 10 minutes or till a toothpick inserted in center comes out clean. Cool 15 minutes on wire rack; remove bread from pan. Cool completely. Makes 1 loaf, about 24 servings.

BREAKFAST PUFFS

Recipes for these tender puffs are in nearly all Amish cookbooks.

1½ cups unbleached flour
1½ teaspoons baking powder
½ teaspoon salt
¼ teaspoon ground mace
½ cup sugar
⅓ cup cooking oil
1 egg
1 teaspoon vanilla
½ cup milk
½ cup sugar
1 teaspoon ground cinnamon
6 tablespoons butter, melted

1. Stir together flour, baking powder, salt and mace. Beat together ½ cup sugar, oil, egg and vanilla with electric mixer on medium speed for 30 seconds. Add flour mixture and milk alternately to egg mixture, beating on low speed after each addition till just combined. Fill 10 greased muffin cups ⅔ full with batter.

2. Bake in a 350° oven for 15 to 20 minutes or till tops of muffins are firm and golden.

3. In shallow bowl, combine ½ cup sugar and cinnamon. While still hot, roll muffins in melted butter, then in cinnamon-sugar mixture. Serve immediately. Makes 10.

HONEY-TOPPED PECAN BREAKFAST BREAD

Though the five daughters of Barbara Dale of Island Lake, Illinois, are grown, they still love their mother's easy-to-make holiday breakfast bread. Baking and eating it is a tradition—usually on Thanksgiving, Christmas and Easter. The women all gather at home to enjoy the warm bread on Christmas morning.

2 8-ounce packages refrigerated crescent rolls
2 tablespoons butter or margarine, melted
½ cup sugar
1 to 2 teaspoons ground cinnamon
¼ cup chopped pecans (optional)
   Honey Topping

1. Unroll crescent-roll dough and divide into 16 triangles. Brush triangles with melted butter or margarine and sprinkle with a mixture of sugar, cinnamon and, if you like, the chopped pecans.

2. Roll up each triangle, starting from the shortest side opposite a point and rolling toward the point. In a greased 9x5x3-inch loaf pan, place 8 of the rolls, point side down. Place remaining rolls on top of the first layer.

3. Bake in a 325° oven for about 55 minutes or till done. Remove bread from pan; turn right side up.

4. Drizzle Honey Topping over the warm bread. Serve warm. Makes 8 servings.

HONEY TOPPING: In a small saucepan, combine ¼ cup sifted *powdered sugar*, 2 tablespoons *honey*, 2 tablespoons *butter* or *margarine* and 1 teaspoon *vanilla*. Heat and stir till mixture is smooth and bubbly. Stir in ¼ cup *pecan halves*. Cool slightly, about 15 minutes, before drizzling over bread.

HOT MUSTARD-CHEESE BREAD

Melted Swiss cheese oozes between mustard-buttered French bread slices in this quick-to-fix bread, contributed by Marlene and Duane Bohrer of Lake Isabel, North Dakota.

6 to 8 slices bacon

1 16-ounce loaf French bread

½ cup butter or margarine, softened

¼ cup chopped green onion or snipped chives

3 tablespoons horseradish mustard

2 teaspoons poppy seed

10 ounces sliced Swiss cheese

1. Crisp-cook and crumble bacon. Cut loaf of bread into 20 slices, cutting to, but not through, bottom crust.

2. Combine butter, onion, mustard, bacon and poppy seed. Spread on both sides of bread slices. Cut cheese slices in half diagonally. Place cheese triangles between bread slices. Wrap bread in foil.

3. Bake in a 350° oven for 20 to 25 minutes. Serve hot. Makes 20 servings.

HOLIDAY MANDEL BREAD

Bakeries in Chicago prepare for Hanukkah with this cookielike bread. It will remind you of the crunchy Italian cookie, biscotti.

¾ cup sugar

¾ cup cooking oil

3 eggs

3 cups all-purpose flour

1 teaspoon baking powder

1 cup chopped nuts

1 cup raisins

2 teaspoons finely shredded lemon peel

1 teaspoon almond extract

1. In a large mixing bowl, combine sugar, cooking oil and eggs, stirring the mixture till the sugar dissolves.

2. In another bowl, mix flour and baking powder. Stir into egg mixture along with chopped nuts, raisins, lemon peel and almond extract (dough will be sticky).

3. Form dough into two 12x3-inch logs on well-greased baking sheet.

4. Bake in a 350° oven 30 minutes.

5. Remove from oven and bias-cut logs into 1-inch slices. Arrange slices on baking sheet.

6. Return to oven and bake for 10 to 12 minutes more. Remove to wire rack to cool. Makes 24 to 28 slices.

PINEAPPLE PANCAKES

Sharon Stilwell of Des Moines created this easy-to-make recipe after canned goods dwindled to just pineapple for the last breakfast on a camping trip.

Cooking oil or bacon fat
1 15¼-ounce can juice-pack pineapple slices (8 slices)
1 6½-ounce packet complete pancake mix
Water or milk
Butter-flavored pancake and waffle syrup

1. Lightly grease hot griddle or heavy skillet with cooking oil or bacon fat. Drain pineapple. Pat pineapple slices with paper towels to remove as much juice as possible.

2. Prepare pancake mix with water or milk, according to package directions. For each pancake, place 1 pineapple slice on griddle. Pour *¼ cup* of the batter over pineapple slice. Cook till golden brown, turning to brown other side when pancakes bubble on the surface and have slightly dry edges. Serve the warm pancakes with butter-flavored syrup. Makes 8 cakes.

GERMAN APPLE PANCAKE

For a weekend breakfast or brunch, delight your family with this puffy pancake. It's from the Apple Haus in Long Grove, Illinois.

¼ cup butter or margarine
2 apples, peeled and thinly sliced
3 eggs
½ cup milk
⅓ cup all-purpose flour
¼ teaspoon salt
¼ cup sugar
½ teaspoon ground cinnamon

1. In a heavy 10-inch ovenproof skillet, heat *2 tablespoons* of the butter or margarine. Add apples and cook over medium heat till apples are just tender, stirring occasionally.

2. For batter, in a blender container, combine eggs, milk, flour and salt. Cover and blend the mixture till it's smooth.

3. Pour the pancake batter over the apples in the skillet. Bake, uncovered, in a 375° oven for 18 minutes or till puffy and golden.

4. Dot the pancake with the remaining butter and sprinkle with the sugar and cinnamon. Return to oven and bake 2 minutes more. Serve pancake immediately. Makes 4 servings.

PIES AND CAKES

Orange Blossom Torte

*White Chocolate Cheesecake
(see recipe, page 155)*

PIES AND CAKES

ORANGE BLOSSOM TORTE

One of the most-requested desserts at Old Rittenhouse Inn in Bayfield, Wisconsin.

9   egg whites
1   cup sugar
9   egg yolks
1   tablespoon lemon juice
1½ cups all-purpose flour
1   ounce white chocolate,
      melted
½   cup butter, melted and
      slightly cooled
    Orange liqueur
    Orange Blossom Filling
    Walnut-Cream Frosting
    Grated orange peel
      (optional)

1. In large mixing bowl, beat egg whites with an electric mixer to soft peaks. Gradually add sugar, beating till stiff peaks form. Set aside. Wash beaters.

2. In small mixing bowl, beat yolks at high speed for 6 minutes or till thick and lemon colored. Add lemon juice. Carefully fold yolk mixture into egg whites. Gradually fold flour into egg mixture. Fold in chocolate and butter.

3. Turn chocolate mixture into two 8x1½-inch round baking pans. Bake in a 325° oven for 30 minutes or till cakes test done. Invert cakes in pans; cool thoroughly.

4. Loosen cakes; remove from pans. Split each layer in half horizontally. Sprinkle each layer with orange liqueur. Spread about ¾ cup Orange Blossom Filling on top of each layer; stack layers. filling side up. Frost sides of torte with Walnut-Cream Frosting. If you like, garnish with orange peel. Makes 8 to 12 servings.

ORANGE BLOSSOM FILLING: In a large mixing bowl, combine ½ cup *dairy sour cream,* one 8-ounce package *cream cheese,* softened, and 1 cup *butter,* softened. Beat till fluffy. Beat in ¼ teaspoon *grated orange peel,* ½ teaspoon *orange extract* and 1 cup sifted *powdered sugar.*

WALNUT-CREAM FROSTING: Combine 1½ cups *whipping cream,* 1 teaspoon *vanilla,* ¼ teaspoon *walnut extract* and a few drops *orange food coloring.* Whip to stiff peaks.

LA BÉCASSE'S NUT TORTE

An ever-changing menu features country French fare at La Bécasse in Burdickville, Michigan. Owner, hostess and dessert chef Peachy Rentenbach, also a ski instructor at nearby Sugar Loaf Mountain, whips up this nutty cake.

1 cup butter or margarine
1 cup sugar
3 eggs
8 ounces finely chopped pecans (2 cups)
⅓ cup cake flour, sifted
1 tablespoon finely shredded lemon peel
Cream-Cheese Filling
Apricot Glaze

1. Generously grease and flour two 8x1½-inch round cake pans. Set aside.

2. In a large mixer bowl, beat the butter with an electric mixer for 30 seconds. Add the sugar and beat till fluffy. Beat in eggs, one at a time.

3. Toss together pecans, cake flour and lemon peel. Stir into egg mixture.

4. Turn batter into prepared pans, smoothing tops with a spatula. Bake in a 350° oven for 30 to 35 minutes or till the cake springs back when lightly touched. Let cool in pans for 10 minutes. Remove from pans; cool completely.

5. Meanwhile, prepare the Cream-Cheese Filling and the Apricot Glaze.

6. To assemble the cake, fill between the layers and ice the sides of the cake with Cream Cheese Filling. Top the cake with the Apricot Glaze. Makes 8 servings.

CREAM-CHEESE FILLING: In a mixing bowl, beat together one 8-ounce package *cream cheese,* softened, ½ cup *sugar* and 1 teaspoon *vanilla* till smooth. Use to fill and ice sides of torte. Makes about 1¼ cups.

APRICOT GLAZE: In a small saucepan, combine one 8-ounce jar *apricot preserves* and 2 tablespoons *dark rum.* Heat till the preserves are melted. Strain and cool slightly. Spread over torte. Makes ¾ cup glaze.

CARAMEL-TOPPED APPLESAUCE CAKE

Gay Coppage took first place at the New Albany, Indiana, Harvest Baking Contest with this eggless cake. Packed with raisins and nuts, it's sure to be a winner at your home.

1   11-ounce package raisins
(2 cups)
Water
1   cup finely chopped black
walnuts or pecans
(8 ounces)
2   tablespoons all-purpose
flour
¾   cup butter or margarine
2   cups sugar
2   cups applesauce
2½ cups all-purpose flour
1   tablespoon ground
cinnamon
1   teaspoon baking soda
1   teaspoon ground nutmeg
Caramel Frosting

1. Place raisins in saucepan. Add enough water to cover. Bring to boiling. Remove from heat and let stand till cool. Drain off the water.

2. Toss the nuts with the 2 tablespoons flour. Set aside.

3. In a mixing bowl, beat the butter or margarine for 30 seconds. Add the sugar and beat till well combined. Beat in applesauce.

4. In another bowl, combine the 2½ cups flour with cinnamon, baking soda and nutmeg. Add to beaten mixture, beating till just combined. Stir in the raisins and nuts.

5. Turn batter into a greased and floured 10-inch tube pan. Bake in 350° oven for 65 to 70 minutes or till done. Cool in pan on rack for 20 minutes. Remove from pan and let cool.

6. Spoon the Caramel Frosting over the cake. Makes 12 servings.

CARAMEL FROSTING: In a medium saucepan, heat ¼ cup *butter* or *margarine* and ½ cup packed *brown sugar* to boiling, stirring occasionally. Remove from heat. Stir in 2 tablespoons *milk* and 1 cup sifted *powdered sugar*. Beat with electric mixer till it's a thick, drizzling consistency. Makes about 1 cup.

Note: For a contrasting chocolate drizzle, melt ½ cup *semisweet chocolate pieces* and drizzle the chocolate over the Caramel Frosting.

HUSKER COLA CAKE

A fan gave this recipe to Nancy Osborne, wife of University of Nebraska football coach, Tom Osborne. It always brings cheers at the coach's house.

2 cups all-purpose flour
2 cups sugar
1 cup cola
½ cup butter or margarine
½ cup shortening
3 tablespoons unsweetened cocoa powder
½ cup buttermilk or sour milk
1 teaspoon baking soda
2 beaten eggs
1 teaspoon vanilla
1½ cups tiny marshmallows
½ cup butter or margarine
⅓ cup cola
1 tablespoon unsweetened cocoa powder
1 16-ounce box powdered sugar, sifted (4½ cups)
1 cup chopped nuts
1 teaspoon vanilla

1. In a large mixing bowl, stir together the flour and sugar.

2. In a saucepan, combine the 1 cup cola, ½ cup butter or margarine, shortening, and 3 tablespoons cocoa powder. Bring the mixture to boiling; stir into the flour and sugar.

3. Stir in the buttermilk, baking soda, eggs, and 1 teaspoon vanilla. Stir in the marshmallows. Turn mixture into a 13x9x2-inch baking pan. Bake in a 350° oven for 30 minutes or till done. Cool in pan on wire rack.

4. Meanwhile, for the frosting: In a saucepan, combine the ½ cup butter or margarine, ⅓ cup cola and 1 tablespoon cocoa powder. Bring to boiling. Remove from heat. Add the sifted powdered sugar, nuts and 1 teaspoon vanilla. Stir till combined. Frost the cake while it's still warm. Makes 12 servings.

Note: To make sour milk, place 1½ teaspoons *lemon juice* or *vinegar* in a glass measuring cup. Add enough *whole milk* to measure ½ cup. Let stand 5 minutes before using.

MAPLE SYRUP CAKE

For years, Roylinda Rumbaugh of Mattawan, Michigan, has been making this cake for holiday gatherings. A sugary crust forms on the buttery, coffee-cakelike dessert as it bakes. You can make it ahead and wrap it up or freeze it for a few days.

2 cups all-purpose flour
2 teaspoons baking powder
½ teaspoon baking soda
½ teaspoon salt
¾ cup sugar
½ cup butter or margarine
2 eggs
½ cup maple-flavored syrup
½ cup milk
¼ cup maple-flavored syrup
1 tablespoon lemon juice

1. Grease and lightly flour a 7- or 8-cup fluted tube mold (also called a Turk's-head mold).

2. In a medium mixing bowl, combine flour, baking powder, baking soda and salt.

3. In a large mixing bowl, beat sugar and butter or margarine with electric mixer till mixture is fluffy. Add eggs, one at a time, beating 1 minute after each. Beat in the ½ cup maple-flavored syrup.

4. Add milk and dry ingredients alternately to egg mixture, beating till just combined after each addition. Pour into mold.

5. Bake in a 350° oven for 40 to 45 minutes or till a toothpick inserted in the center comes out clean. Cool cake in pan on a wire rack for 10 minutes.

6. Meanwhile, in a small bowl, stir together ¼ cup maple-flavored syrup and the lemon juice.

7. Remove the cake from pan. Prick the top of the cake with a fork. Pour the syrup mixture over the warm cake. Cool. Makes 12 servings.

ORANGE-SLICE GUMDROP CAKE

Generations of Mary E. Francis' family, from her grandmother to her grandchildren, prefer this moist, sweet version of fruitcake to the more traditional one. Mary also bakes her cake as a holiday gift for lucky friends and neighbors in Rapid City, South Dakota.

1 cup butter or margarine
4 eggs
1 pound orange slice-shaped gumdrops, cut up (3 cups)
½ cup all-purpose flour
2 cups sugar
3 cups all-purpose flour
1 cup buttermilk or sour milk
1 8-ounce package pitted dates, cut up (1⅓ cups)
1 7-ounce package flaked coconut (2⅔ cups)
2 cups chopped nuts
    Orange Glaze

1. Let butter and eggs stand at room temperature for 30 minutes. Toss together gumdrops and the ½ cup flour. Set aside.

2. In an extra-large mixing bowl, beat butter with an electric mixer for 30 seconds. Gradually add sugar, beating well. Add eggs, one at a time, beating for 1 minute after each addition and scraping bowl frequently.

3. Add the 3 cups flour and buttermilk alternately to beaten mixture, beating after each addition till just combined. Fold in dates, coconut and nuts. Fold in gumdrop mixture.

4. Spoon batter into 2 greased and floured 9x5x3-inch loaf pans that have been lined with waxed paper, or 2 greased and floured 6-cup fluted tube pans or ring molds. Spread batter evenly in pans.

5. Bake in a 300° oven 1 hour and 40 minutes or till a toothpick inserted near the center comes out clean.

6. Pour Orange Glaze over hot fruitcakes. Cool in pans on wire rack for 20 minutes.

7. Remove from pans and discard waxed paper. Cool completely on wire racks. Wrap in clear plastic wrap. Store in the refrigerator for up to 4 weeks. Bring to room temperature before serving. Makes 2 fruitcakes.

ORANGE GLAZE: In a small mixing bowl, stir together 2 cups sifted *powdered sugar* and ½ cup *orange juice.*

CHUNKY CHOCOLATE FRUITCAKE

Unlike the proverbial fruitcake that seems to last forever, this tasty chocolate version will disappear fast. A friend of Ruth Ippel of Sheboygan, Wisconsin, gave her the recipe when that woman and Ruth both were newlyweds more than 40 years ago. It's packed with chocolate, nuts and fruit.

1	8-ounce package pitted dates, snipped (1⅓ cups)
½	cup candied red or green cherries
½	cup sugar
⅔	cup all-purpose flour
1	teaspoon baking powder
¼	teaspoon salt
2	egg yolks
2	tablespoons water
6	ounces semisweet chocolate, chopped (6 squares)
2	cups walnut halves (8 ounces)
1¾	cups Brazil nuts (8 ounces)
2	egg whites
	Candied cherry halves (optional)
	Melted semisweet chocolate (optional)

1. Grease four 5½x3x2-inch loaf pans or one 9x5x3-inch loaf pan. Line bottom and sides with brown paper; grease paper. Set aside.

2. In a large bowl, combine dates, cherries and sugar. Mix till fruit is well coated with sugar.

3. Stir together flour, baking powder and salt. Add to fruit and mix well.

4. Combine egg yolks and water. Stir into fruit mixture (mixture will be sticky). Add the 6 ounces of chocolate and the nuts. Mix well to evenly coat fruit and nuts.

5. Beat egg whites till stiff peaks form (tips stand straight). Add to fruit-and-nut mixture, stirring to coat the fruit and nuts evenly with the batter. Spoon mixture into prepared pans. Press down with back of a spoon.

6. Bake in a 300° oven for about 35 minutes for small loaves or 65 minutes for large loaf or till golden brown.

7. Cool in pans on wire rack. Remove from pans. Remove and discard paper. Wrap in plastic wrap or bag and store for 3 to 4 months in the refrigerator or 1 year in the freezer. For garnish, top with candied cherry halves and drizzle with melted semisweet chocolate, if you like. Makes 4 small loaves or 1 large loaf.

PUMPKIN-PRALINE LAYER CAKE

Mother and daughter Diane and Julie Weer both entered winning recipes in the bake-off at the Morton, Illinois, pumpkin festival. "I couldn't believe we both won!" says Diane, who baked this cake.

1 cup packed brown sugar
½ cup margarine
¼ cup whipping cream
¾ cup chopped pecans
2 cups all-purpose flour
2 teaspoons baking powder
2 teaspoons pumpkin pie
    spice
1 teaspoon baking soda
1 teaspoon salt
1⅔ cups sugar
1 cup cooking oil
4 eggs
2 cups canned pumpkin
¼ teaspoon black walnut
    flavoring (optional)
  Whipped Cream
    Topping

1. In a heavy saucepan, combine brown sugar, margarine and whipping cream. Cook over low heat just till sugar dissolves, stirring occasionally. Pour the mixture into two 9x1½-inch round baking pans. Sprinkle evenly with pecans. Let the mixture cool slightly.

2. Stir together flour, baking powder, pie spice, soda and salt. Set aside. In a large mixing bowl, beat together sugar, oil and eggs. Add pumpkin and dry ingredients alternately to oil mixture, beating till just combined. Stir in black walnut flavoring, if you like.

3. Carefully spoon batter over the pecan/brown-sugar mixture in the baking pans. Place pans on a baking sheet. Bake in a 350° oven for 35 to 40 minutes or till cake tests done. Cool in pans on wire racks for 5 minutes. Invert onto wire racks, replacing any topping that remains in pan. Cool completely.

4. To assemble cake, place 1 cake layer on a serving plate, praline side up. Spread with Whipped Cream Topping. Top with second layer, praline side up. Pipe or dollop with the remaining topping. Makes 10 to 12 servings.

WHIPPED CREAM TOPPING: Beat 1¾ cups *whipping cream* with an electric mixer till soft peaks form (tips curl). Add ¼ cup sifted *powdered sugar* and ¼ teaspoon *vanilla*. Beat till stiff peaks form (tips stand straight).

Note: Assemble the cake no more than 1½ hours before serving. Keep chilled until served.

PASSOVER CHOCO-NUT CAKE

The ingredients meet Passover restrictions, but you don't have to wait for the holiday to bake this rich flour-free cake that's a specialty of Sharon Winstein of St. Louis.

10 to 12 egg whites
      (about 1½ cups)
10 to 12 egg yolks
 3 squares (3 ounces)
      unsweetened chocolate
½ cup semisweet chocolate
      pieces
⅔ cup sugar
 2 cups very finely chopped
      almonds or pecans
¾ teaspoon pure vanilla
¼ teaspoon almond extract
¼ cup sugar
 1 cup semisweet chocolate
      pieces
 1 teaspoon butter or
      margarine
½ teaspoon instant coffee
      crystals
 1 tablespoon hot water
 3 tablespoons dairy sour
      cream
¼ teaspoon maple flavoring

1. Let egg whites and yolks stand, covered, at room temperature for 30 minutes. In a small, heavy saucepan, partially melt unsweetened chocolate and ½ cup chocolate pieces over low heat. Turn off heat and stir till melted.

2. Cut a waxed-paper liner for the bottom of a 10-inch tube pan, cutting it ½ inch wider than the pan. Grease pan thoroughly. Place liner in pan and grease liner.

3. Beat yolks with an electric mixer on high speed for about 4 minutes or till thick and lemon-colored. Add ⅔ cup sugar, beating till very thick. Stir in melted chocolate and nuts.

4. Thoroughly wash and dry beaters. Beat egg whites with vanilla and almond extract till foamy. Gradually add ¼ cup sugar to egg whites, beating till soft peaks form (tips curl). Lighten yolk mixture with about 2 cups beaten whites. Fold into remaining white mixture. Turn batter into prepared pan.

5. Bake in a 350° oven for about 40 minutes or till top springs back when lightly touched. Loosen from edge and center of pan. Cool in pan for 1 hour. Invert onto cake plate. Remove waxed paper.

6. To prepare glaze, melt 1 cup chocolate pieces over low heat. Remove from heat; stir in butter. Dissolve coffee crystals in hot water. Stir in sour cream and maple flavoring. Add sour-cream mixture to chocolate, stirring till smooth and shiny. Spread glaze over top and sides of cake. Makes 10 to 15 servings.

CHEESECAKE-MINCEMEAT PIE

Restaurants at Branson, Missouri's Silver Dollar City theme park serve this layered treat.

1½ cups prepared mincemeat
⅓ cup chopped walnuts
1 baked 9-inch pie shell
1 8-ounce package and one
    3-ounce package
    cream cheese, softened
2 eggs
⅓ cup sugar
1 tablespoon milk
¾ cup dairy sour cream
2 tablespoons sugar
½ teaspoon vanilla
¼ cup chopped walnuts

1. Combine the mincemeat and ⅓ cup walnuts. Spoon mixture into cooled, baked pie shell and spread evenly.

2. In a mixing bowl, beat cream cheese, eggs, ⅓ cup sugar and milk till smooth. Pour over mincemeat and spread evenly. Bake in a 375° oven about 25 minutes or till nearly set.

3. Combine sour cream, 2 tablespoons sugar and vanilla. Spread over pie. Sprinkle with remaining nuts. Bake 5 minutes more. Cool. Chill 5 hours before serving. Makes 1 pie.

AMISH VANILLA PIE

Creamy with a definite crunch, this molasses-sweet dessert comes from the Indiana Amish.

1 egg
1 tablespoon all-purpose
    flour
½ cup packed brown sugar
½ cup light molasses
1 cup water
1 teaspoon vanilla
¼ teaspoon ground mace
⅛ teaspoon salt
1 unbaked 9-inch pie shell
1 cup all-purpose flour
½ cup packed brown sugar
1 teaspoon vanilla
½ teaspoon cream of tartar
½ teaspoon baking soda
¼ teaspoon ground mace
⅛ teaspoon salt
¼ cup cold butter

1. In a medium saucepan, beat egg till frothy. Stir in 1 tablespoon flour. Add brown sugar, molasses, water, 1 teaspoon vanilla, mace and salt; mix well. Over medium-high heat, bring mixture to a full rolling boil, stirring occasionally. Remove mixture from heat; cool. (The filling will be slightly thickened.)

2. Place unbaked pie shell on oven rack. Pour filling into the pastry shell.

3. To prepare topping, mix remaining ingredients *except* butter. Cut in butter till pieces resemble coarse crumbs. Sprinkle topping over filling. Cover edge of pastry with foil.

4. Bake in a 350° oven for 25 minutes; remove foil. Bake 20 minutes more or till top is deep, golden brown. Filling will be a bit soft. Cool completely before cutting. Makes 1 pie.

STRAWBERRY CREAM PIE

This berry delight is a summer sensation from Leigh Ann Kloefkorn of Wichita, Kansas.

1¾ cups flaked coconut
¼ cup butter or margarine, melted
3 cups fresh strawberries, chopped
¾ cup sugar
1 envelope unflavored gelatin
¼ cup cold water
2 teaspoons lemon juice
1½ cups whipping cream
1 cup fresh strawberries

1. In a bowl, combine coconut and melted butter or margarine. Press onto bottom and up sides of a 9-inch pie plate. Bake in a 300° oven for 20 to 25 minutes or till just golden. Cool.

2. In a bowl, combine chopped strawberries and sugar. Set aside for about 10 minutes or till the sugar dissolves. In a small saucepan, soften gelatin in cold water for 1 minute. Stir over low heat till gelatin dissolves; cool slightly. Add to berry mixture with lemon juice.

3. Whip *1 cup* of the whipping cream. Fold into strawberry mixture. Chill till mixture mounds when dropped from a spoon. Spoon strawberry mixture into cooled piecrust. Cover and chill for at least 4 hours or till set. To serve, whip the remaining ½ cup whipping cream. Garnish the pie with the whipped cream and 1 cup strawberries. Makes 1 pie.

STRAWBERRY LOVER'S PIE

Chocolate and strawberry blend deliciously in this pie from Joyce Fulton of Troy, Ohio.

2 squares semisweet chocolate (2 ounces)
1 tablespoon butter
1 baked 9-inch pie shell
2 3-ounce packages cream cheese, softened
½ cup dairy sour cream
2 to 3 tablespoons sugar
½ teaspoon vanilla
3 to 4 cups hulled fresh strawberries
⅓ cup strawberry jam

1. Melt chocolate and butter over low heat, stirring occasionally. Spread evenly over the bottom and sides of cooled, baked pie shell.

2. In a mixing bowl, beat together cream cheese, sour cream, sugar and vanilla till smooth. Spread evenly in pie shell. Cover and chill at least 2 hours.

3. Before serving, arrange berries, hulled end down, over cream cheese filling. Heat the strawberry jam till just melted. Add some *water* till thin. Drizzle over the arranged strawberries in the pie. Makes 1 pie.

CHERRY-ALMOND PIE

Here's a delicious new twist on cherry pie—a classic Midwest dessert.

5 cups fresh or frozen
    unsweetened, pitted,
    tart red cherries
  Pastry for a double-crust
    9-inch pie
¾ to 1 cup sugar
⅓ cup chopped almonds,
    toasted
3 tablespoons quick-
    cooking tapioca
1 tablespoon Amaretto or
    several drops almond
    extract

1. Thaw cherries, if frozen. Prepare pastry; shape into 2 balls. Flatten the dough slightly.

2. Combine the thawed cherries with sugar, almonds, tapioca and Amaretto. Let the fruit-and-nut mixture stand for 10 minutes.

3. On a lightly floured surface, roll each ball of pastry to form a 12-inch circle. Carefully ease one portion of the pastry into a 9-inch pie plate. Trim pastry even with edges of pie plate. Cut decorative slits in remaining rolled pastry.

4. Turn filling into the pie plate. Add pastry for the top crust; trim ½-inch beyond the edge of the pie plate. Flute the edge. Cover the edge of the pie with foil. Place on a baking sheet. Bake the pie in a 400° oven for 30 minutes; remove foil. Bake for 15 to 20 minutes more or till golden. Cool on wire rack. Makes 1 pie.

GERMAN CHOCOLATE PIE

At holiday time, Kansas Governor Joan Finney whips up this decadent pie.

1 4-ounce package German
    sweet chocolate
¼ cup butter or margarine
1 12-ounce can evaporated
    milk (1⅔ cups)
1½ cups sugar
3 tablespoons cornstarch
⅛ teaspoon salt
2 slightly beaten eggs
1 teaspoon vanilla
1 unbaked 9-inch pie shell
1⅓ cups coconut
½ cup chopped nuts

1. In a heavy, small saucepan, heat and stir chocolate and butter over low heat till melted. Remove from heat. Stir evaporated milk into the melted chocolate mixture. Combine sugar, cornstarch and salt. Stir in eggs and vanilla. Stir chocolate mixture into egg mixture. Pour into unbaked pie shell. Combine coconut and nuts. Sprinkle over filling in the shell.

2. Bake in a 375° oven for 25 minutes. Cover with foil; continue baking for 25 to 30 minutes more or till puffed and browned. (Filling will be soft.) Let cool, then chill for at least 4 hours or till serving time. Makes 1 pie.

LEMON SPONGE PIE

Marcia Adams, author of "Cooking from Quilt Country," has collected numerous Amish recipes. She credits this version of an Amish favorite to Indiana resident Lizzie Yoder. Lizzie says, "I always fix these pies when our relatives come out to visit from Iowa. They don't make this kind of lemon pie there." What makes this pie unique is its delicate top layer above a lemon-custard filling.

Pastry for a single-crust 9-inch pie
1 **cup sugar**
2 **teaspoons finely shredded lemon peel**
3 **egg yolks**
3 **tablespoons all-purpose flour**
1 **tablespoon butter, softened**
⅛ **teaspoon salt**
⅓ **cup lemon juice**
1 **cup milk**
3 **egg whites**

1. On a lightly floured surface, roll out pie pastry to form a 12-inch circle. Ease the rolled pastry into a 9-inch pie plate. Trim the pastry to ½-inch beyond rim. Flute edge of the crust. Don't prick the pastry. Line pastry with a double thickness of heavy foil. Bake in a 375° oven for 10 minutes. Remove foil; bake 5 minutes more. Remove the crust from the oven and set aside. Reduce the oven temperature to 325°.

2. In a large mixing bowl, beat sugar, shredded lemon peel, egg yolks, flour, butter and salt with electric mixer till well blended. Add the lemon juice and beat till well blended. Beat in milk. Wash beaters thoroughly.

3. In small mixing bowl, beat egg whites till stiff peaks form (tips stand straight). Fold into the lemon mixture. This is a thin mixture and will look a bit like a lemon soufflé on top with some flecks of white still remaining. Place pre-baked pie shell on oven rack. Pour filling into the pie shell.

4. Bake the pie in a 325° oven about 35 minutes or till the top is golden and appears set. The pie filling will still be shaky, but will firm up as it cools. Do not overbake or the custard will "weep." Cool completely on a wire rack before cutting. Makes 1 pie.

PARADISE PUMPKIN PIE

"This pie is a combination of recipes I put together," says Eileen Bogar of Minier, Illinois.

1   8-ounce package cream
    cheese, softened
¼   cup sugar
½   teaspoon vanilla
1   slightly beaten egg
1   unbaked 9-inch pie shell
1¼ cups canned pumpkin
1   cup evaporated milk
2   beaten eggs
¼   cup packed brown sugar
¼   cup sugar
1   teaspoon ground
    cinnamon
2   tablespoons butter
¼   teaspoon ground nutmeg
½   cup chopped pecans
2   tablespoons all-purpose
    flour
2   tablespoons brown sugar

1. In a small mixing bowl, beat together the cream cheese, ¼ cup sugar, vanilla and the 1 egg till smooth. Chill for 30 minutes. Turn into unbaked pie shell.

2. Combine pumpkin, milk, the 2 eggs, ¼ cup brown sugar, ¼ cup sugar, cinnamon, nutmeg and ¼ teaspoon *salt*. Carefully pour over cream cheese mixture.

3. Cover edge of the pie with foil. Bake in a 350° oven for 25 minutes. Remove foil; bake 25 minutes more.

4. Meanwhile, soften butter. Combine butter, pecans, flour and 2 tablespoons brown sugar. Sprinkle over pie. Bake for 10 to 15 minutes more or till a knife inserted near the center comes out clean. Cool on rack. Makes 1 pie.

BLACK WALNUT-OATMEAL PIE

Oatmeal is the unusual ingredient in this Midwest Amish cousin of the pecan pie.

3   slightly beaten eggs
1   cup packed brown sugar
½   cup dark corn syrup
½   cup evaporated milk
½   cup quick-cooking rolled
    oats
½   cup coarsely chopped
    black walnuts
¼   cup butter, melted
1   teaspoon vanilla
1   unbaked 9-inch pie shell

1. In a large mixing bowl, combine eggs, sugar, syrup, milk, oats, nuts, butter, vanilla and ⅛ teaspoon *salt;* mix well.

2. Place unbaked pie shell on oven rack; pour in filling. Cover edge of pie with foil.

3. Bake in a 350° oven for 25 minutes; remove foil. Bake about 25 minutes more or till top is deep, golden brown and a bit puffy. Filling will still be a bit soft, but will firm up as it cools. Cool completely. Makes 1 pie.

MAPLE-NUT PIE

This Heartland version of pecan pie uses maple syrup from the north woods.

Pastry for a single-crust
9-inch pie
⅓ cup packed brown sugar
2 tablespoons all-purpose
flour
3 eggs
1 cup pure maple syrup
2 tablespoons butter or
margarine, melted
1 teaspoon vanilla
Dash salt
½ cup chopped pecans

1. Prepare and roll out pastry. Line a 9-inch pie plate. Trim pastry to ½-inch beyond edge of pie plate. Flute edge; do not prick pastry. Bake in 450° oven for 5 minutes. (Pastry may puff slightly.) Cool thoroughly on a wire rack.

2. For filling, combine brown sugar and flour. Beat eggs slightly with rotary beater or fork. Stir in flour mixture, maple syrup, melted butter or margarine, vanilla and salt; beat with rotary beater just till smooth. Stir in pecans.

3. Place pie shell on oven rack; pour filling into the partially baked pastry shell. Cover edge of pie with foil. Bake in 350° oven for 25 minutes. Remove foil; bake for 15 to 20 minutes more or till knife inserted off-center comes out clean. Cool pie thoroughly on rack. Cover and chill to store. Makes 1 pie.

MYSTERY PECAN PIE

Marilyn Zmudzinski of Harrietta, Michigan, contributes this irresistible double-layer treat that combines two favorites: cheesecake and pecan pie.

1 8-ounce package cream
cheese, softened
⅓ cup sugar
1 teaspoon vanilla
⅛ teaspoon salt
1 egg
1 unbaked 9-inch pie shell
1¼ cups chopped pecans
2 slightly beaten eggs
⅔ cup light corn syrup
¼ cup sugar
1 teaspoon vanilla

1. Combine cream cheese, ⅓ cup sugar, 1 teaspoon vanilla and salt. Beat with an electric mixer till smooth. Add 1 egg and beat on low speed till mixture is combined. Spread mixture over bottom of the unbaked pie shell. Sprinkle pecans evenly over cream cheese mixture.

2. Mix 2 eggs, corn syrup, ¼ cup sugar and 1 teaspoon vanilla. Carefully pour over pecans.

3. Bake in a 375° oven for 40 to 45 minutes or till puffed and center appears nearly set when you shake it. Cool completely on a wire rack. Store in refrigerator. Makes 1 pie.

APPLE-CRANBERRY PIE

This sweet-tart pie comes from the New Albany, Indiana, Harvest Baking Contest.

Pastry for a double-crust
    9-inch pie
¾ cup packed brown sugar
¼ to ½ cup sugar
⅓ cup all-purpose flour
1 teaspoon ground
    cinnamon
4 cups sliced cooking
    apples (such as
    Jonathan, Winesap or
    Golden Delicious)
2 cups fresh or frozen
    cranberries (whole or
    chopped)
2 tablespoons butter or
    margarine

1. Prepare the pastry and divide into 2 portions. On a lightly floured surface, roll out one portion of pastry. Fit into a 9-inch pie plate. Trim pastry ½-inch beyond edge of pie plate. Roll out remaining pastry for top crust. Cover and set aside.

2. In a large bowl, toss together the sugars, flour and cinnamon. Add apples and cranberries; mix well. Turn into pastry-lined pie plate.

3. Dot mixture with butter or margarine. Cover with top crust, cutting slits so steam can escape. Seal the top crust and flute the edges.

4. Cover edge of pie with foil. Bake in a 375° oven for 25 minutes. Remove foil; bake 20 to 25 minutes more. Cool on rack. Makes 1 pie.

PREGNANT-WOMAN PIE

According to the staff at the Minnesota Forest History Center (near Grand Rapids), logging camp cooks jokingly named this pie after the dried apples that swell as they cook.

6 cups water
3 6-ounce packages dried
    apples
Pastry for a double-crust
    9-inch pie
¼ cup packed brown sugar
2 tablespoons all-purpose
    flour
1 teaspoon ground
    cinnamon
½ teaspoon ground allspice
1 tablespoon butter

1. In a 4-quart Dutch oven, combine water and the dried apples; bring to boiling and reduce heat. Cover and simmer for 35 to 45 minutes or till the liquid is absorbed. Meanwhile, line a 9-inch pie plate with half the pastry. Trim pastry even with the rim.

2. Mix brown sugar, flour, cinnamon and allspice. Toss with cooked apples. Turn into the pastry-lined pie plate. Dot with butter. Position and adjust top crust; cut slits in top. Seal and flute the edge. Cover edge with foil.

3. Bake in a 375° oven for 20 minutes; remove foil. Continue baking for 20 to 25 minutes more or till crust is golden. Cool. Makes 1 pie.

COOKIES
AND
CANDIES

Ruth's Peppermint Pinwheels

*Irma's Frosted
Eggnog Logs*

COOKIES AND CANDIES

RUTH'S PEPPERMINT PINWHEELS

Ruth Lewis first brought this yuletide treat to the Minocqua, Wisconsin, cookie walk. She's since moved to Michigan, but her cookies remain a favorite.

2½ cups all-purpose flour
¼ teaspoon salt
1 cup butter or margarine
1 cup sifted powdered
     sugar
1 egg
1 teaspoon vanilla
1 teaspoon almond extract
     or ¾ teaspoon
     peppermint extract
½ teaspoon red food
     coloring
1 egg white
1 tablespoon water
¼ cup finely crushed
     peppermint candy

1. Stir together the flour and salt.

2. In a mixing bowl, beat butter or margarine for 30 seconds. Beat in powdered sugar till fluffy. Add egg, vanilla and almond or peppermint extract; beat well. Add the dry ingredients. Beat till just combined.

3. Divide dough in half. Mix red food coloring in one-half of dough. Chill doughs 1 hour or till easy to handle.

4. On lightly floured surface, divide each portion of dough in half. Roll out each of the 4 balls of dough to form an 8-inch square.

5. Place a white square of cookie dough on top of a red square of cookie dough. Roll up, jelly-roll style. Repeat with remaining dough. Wrap the cookie-dough rolls in waxed paper and chill for 2 to 24 hours.

6. To bake, cut dough into ¼-inch-thick slices. Place on ungreased cookie sheets. Bake in a 375° oven for 8 to 10 minutes or till edges are firm and bottoms are light brown. Remove cookies and cool on wire racks.

7. Beat together the egg white and water. Brush egg white mixture over warm cookies. Sprinkle with finely crushed peppermint candy. Makes about 60 cookies.

Note: If you use corn-oil margarine, chill the dough in the freezer for 2 to 24 hours.

ORANGE COOKIES

"Pay attention to the baking time and don't go over or under," Rhoda Ackels warns. This veteran Howell, Michigan, baker always has a full cookie jar on hand.

1⅓ cups all-purpose flour
 ½ teaspoon baking powder
 ¼ teaspoon baking soda
 ½ cup sugar
 3 tablespoons shortening
 3 tablespoons butter or margarine
 1 egg
 ⅓ cup buttermilk
 1 teaspoon finely shredded orange peel
 2 tablespoons orange juice
    Orange Icing

1. Stir together the flour, baking powder and baking soda. Set aside. Beat together sugar, shortening and butter. Add egg; beat till fluffy. Beat in buttermilk, peel and orange juice. Add dry ingredients; beat till combined.

2. Drop by teaspoonfuls onto ungreased cookie sheets. Bake in 350° oven 10 minutes. Remove; cool on racks. Prepare Orange Icing. Frost cookies. Makes about 30 cookies.

ORANGE ICING: Beat together 2 cups sifted *powdered sugar*, 2 teaspoons finely shredded *orange peel* and 2 to 3 tablespoons *orange juice* to make a spreadable, thick frosting.

SPICY PUMPKIN COOKIES

A brown-sugar glaze tops these cakelike pumpkin cookies, which took first place in the children's cookie category at the Harvest Baking Contest in New Albany, Indiana.

1 cup shortening
1 cup sugar
1 cup canned pumpkin
1 egg
2 cups all-purpose flour
1 tablespoon pumpkin-pie spice
½ teaspoon baking powder
¼ teaspoon baking soda
   Cookie Glaze

1. In an extra-large mixing bowl, beat shortening and sugar till fluffy. Beat in pumpkin and egg. Combine flour, spice, baking powder and soda. Beat into the pumpkin mixture.

2. Spoon by rounded teaspoonfuls onto ungreased cookie sheets. Bake in a 375° oven for 8 to 10 minutes or till the tops seem firm. Remove; cool on wire racks. Spread Cookie Glaze over cookies. Makes 42 to 48 cookies.

COOKIE GLAZE: In saucepan, combine ½ cup packed *brown sugar*, 3 tablespoons *butter* and 1 tablespoon *milk*. Heat and stir till butter melts. Remove from heat. Stir in 1 cup sifted *powdered sugar* and 1 teaspoon *vanilla*. (If too thick, stir in a few drops of hot water.)

NUTBUTTER DREAMS

Sharon Lee Puttmann of Rice Lake, Wisconsin, says, "I bought this sesame seed butter and I didn't know what to do with it." We think her cookies are the perfect answer.

1½   cups all-purpose flour
½   cup packed brown sugar
½   teaspoon baking soda
¼   teaspoon salt
½   cup shortening
½   cup sesame, cashew or almond butter
¼   cup honey
1   tablespoon milk
1   teaspoon vanilla

1. Combine flour, brown sugar, soda and salt. Cut in shortening till mixture resembles coarse crumbs. Cut in your choice of butter. Stir together the honey, milk and vanilla. Add to flour mixture; mix well.

2. Shape dough into 1½-inch balls. Place on lightly greased cookie sheets. Flatten slightly with sugared glass. Bake in a 350° oven 10 to 12 minutes. Let stand 1 minute. Remove; cool on wire racks. Makes 30 cookies.

LEMON LASSIES

"Make sure the dough is well chilled," advises Lorraine Horner of Minneapolis, Kansas.

2¼   cups all-purpose flour
1   teaspoon ground cinnamon
½   teaspoon baking soda
¼   teaspoon salt
1   cup sugar
½   cup butter or margarine
1   egg
¼   cup molasses
½   cup sugar
2   eggs
1   tablespoon grated lemon peel
¼   cup lemon juice
⅛   teaspoon salt
1   cup coconut

1. Combine first 4 ingredients. Set aside. Beat together 1 cup sugar and butter till light. Add 1 egg and molasses. Beat till fluffy. Stir in dry ingredients. Cover; chill 1 hour.

2. For filling, in a saucepan, combine the ½ cup sugar, 2 eggs, peel, juice and ⅛ teaspoon salt. Cook and stir over medium heat till thickened and bubbly. Cook and stir 1 minute more. Stir in coconut. Cover and chill.

3. Divide dough into 4 parts; roll each into a 15-inch-long rope. Flatten each rope to form a 15x3-inch rectangle. Spread filling evenly lengthwise down center of rectangles. Fold sides of dough over filling, overlapping slightly and sealing. Place seams side down. Flatten slightly. Cut crosswise into 1½-inch bars. Place on ungreased cookie sheets. Bake in a 350° oven 12 to 15 minutes or till set. Remove; cool on racks. Makes 40 cookies.

CHEESECAKE COOKIES

For a decorative touch, Karen Flemal of Sun Prairie, Wisconsin, sometimes cuts her rich cookies into triangular shapes.

5 tablespoons butter
⅓ cup packed brown sugar
1 cup all-purpose flour
¼ cup chopped walnuts
1 8-ounce package cream cheese
½ cup sugar
1 egg
2 tablespoons milk
1 to 2 tablespoons lemon juice
½ teaspoon vanilla

1. Beat butter for 30 seconds to soften. Add the brown sugar and beat till fluffy. Beat in flour and nuts. Set aside 1 cup of this mixture. Press remaining mixture into bottom of ungreased 8x8x2-inch baking pan. Bake in a 350° oven 12 minutes.

2. Meanwhile, beat together the cream cheese and sugar. Mix in egg, milk, lemon juice and vanilla. Pour over baked layer. Sprinkle reserved butter mixture over top. Bake in 350° oven 25 minutes. Cool; cut into bars. Store, covered, in the refrigerator. Makes 28 bars.

ZINGY ZUCCHINI BARS

The fruit and frosting make these bars from North Dakotan Marlene Bohrer memorable.

1¾ cups all-purpose flour
1½ teaspoons baking powder
1 teaspoon salt
¾ cup butter or margarine
½ cup sugar
½ cup packed brown sugar
2 eggs
½ teaspoon vanilla
2 cups shredded zucchini
¾ cup coconut
¾ cup snipped, pitted dates
¾ cup raisins
Cinnamon Frosting

1. Grease a 15x10x1-inch baking pan. Stir together flour, baking powder and salt. In a large mixing bowl, beat butter, sugar and brown sugar with electric mixer till well combined. Beat in eggs and vanilla. Add flour mixture; beat on low speed till combined (batter will be thick). By hand, stir in zucchini, coconut, dates and raisins. Spread in pan.

2. Bake in a 350° oven for 30 to 40 minutes or till wooden toothpick inserted near center comes out clean. Cool. Frost with Cinnamon Frosting. Makes about 36 bars.

CINNAMON FROSTING: Beat together two 3-ounce packages *cream cheese,* ½ cup *butter,* 2 teaspoons *vanilla* and ¾ teaspoon ground *cinnamon* till fluffy. Gradually beat in 4 cups sifted *powdered sugar.* If necessary, add a little more powdered sugar or milk.

CHOCOLATE-FILLED COOKIES

Janet Summers of McPherson, Kansas, calls these bars "super-easy and super-delicious."

1 cup butter or margarine
2 cups all-purpose flour
½ cup sugar
⅛ teaspoon salt
1 14-ounce can sweetened
    condensed milk
1 6-ounce package
    semisweet chocolate
    pieces (1 cup)
½ cup chopped walnuts
½ teaspoon vanilla

1. Beat butter or margarine with an electric mixer on low speed for 30 seconds. Add flour, sugar and salt; beat on low speed till combined. Press ⅔ of the mixture into the bottom of an ungreased 13x9x2-inch baking pan.

2. In a medium saucepan, combine condensed milk and chocolate. Stir over low heat till chocolate melts and mixture is smooth. Remove from heat. Stir in nuts and vanilla. Spread hot mixture over the crust. Dot with remaining crust mixture.

3. Bake in 350° oven about 35 minutes or till golden. Cool on wire rack. Makes 48 squares.

MAPLE NUTTY BARS

These easy-to-make cookies from Barbara Ward of Wabash, Indiana, yield a bunch.

12 ounces chocolate-
    flavored candy coating
3 cups salted peanuts
1 12-ounce package butter-
    scotch pieces (2 cups)
1 12-ounce jar peanut
    butter (1¼ cups)
1 cup butter or margarine
½ cup evaporated milk
1 4-serving-size package
    regular vanilla
    pudding mix
1 tablespoon maple
    flavoring
1 teaspoon vanilla
2 pounds sifted powdered
    sugar (8 to 9 cups)

1. Cut up candy coating. Chop peanuts. In a heavy medium saucepan, combine candy coating and butterscotch pieces. Cook and stir over low heat till melted. Stir in peanut butter. Spread *1¾ cups* of the mixture into a greased 15x10x1-inch baking pan. Refrigerate till mixture in pan is set (about 20 minutes). Set remaining mixture aside.

2. In large saucepan, melt butter. Stir in evaporated milk and pudding mix. Cook and stir over medium heat till thickened. (Mixture may appear curdled.) Stir in maple flavoring and vanilla. Stir in powdered sugar. Carefully spread over cooled mixture in pan. If necessary, reheat remaining chocolate mixture to melt. Stir in peanuts. Carefully spread over pudding. Chill to set. Makes about 60 squares.

IRMA'S FROSTED EGGNOG LOGS

This nutmeg cookie with rum-flavored frosting will remind you of eggnog. Irma Biek of Minocqua, Wisconsin, always includes it in her holiday-season baking spree.

3 cups all-purpose flour
1 teaspoon ground nutmeg
1 cup butter or margarine
¾ cup sugar
1 egg
2 teaspoons vanilla
1 teaspoon rum flavoring
   Rum Frosting

1. In a mixing bowl, stir together the flour and ground nutmeg.

2. In a large mixing bowl, beat butter for 30 seconds. Add sugar and beat till fluffy. Beat in the egg, vanilla and rum flavoring till combined. Add dry ingredients; beat well.

3. Shape cookie dough into 3-inch-long logs, about ½-inch wide. Arrange logs on ungreased cookie sheets.

4. Bake in a 350° oven for 15 to 17 minutes or till golden. Remove and cool on wire racks.

5. Frost tops of the cooled cookies with the Rum Frosting. Mark frosting lengthwise with tines of a fork to resemble bark. Sprinkle with additional nutmeg. Makes about 54 cookies.

RUM FROSTING: In a mixing bowl, beat together 3 tablespoons softened *butter* or *margarine*, ½ teaspoon *rum flavoring* and ½ teaspoon *vanilla*. Beat in ½ cup sifted *powdered sugar*. Gradually add more sifted powdered sugar (about 2 cups) and 2 to 3 tablespoons *evaporated milk, cream* or *milk,* beating till the frosting spreads easily over the cookies. Tint the frosting with *food coloring,* if you like.

SOUR CREAM-AND-NUTMEG SOFTIES

Ardith Fischer's family in Owen, Wisconsin, loves thick, soft sugar cookies. Though Ardith never found the recipe for her grandmother's cookies, which she always remembered, this one comes close. Because today's cookie cutters don't produce giant cookies, Ardith improvises with a carefully washed vegetable or fruit can.

4	cups all-purpose flour
1	teaspoon baking soda
1	teaspoon ground nutmeg
½	teaspoon salt
½	cup butter or margarine
½	cup lard or shortening
1½	cups sugar
1	egg
1	cup dairy sour cream
1	teaspoon vanilla
	Powdered Sugar Icing (optional)
	Colored sugar or decorative candies (optional)

1. Stir together flour, baking soda, nutmeg and salt. Set aside.

2. In a large mixing bowl, beat butter or margarine and lard or shortening till softened. Add sugar and beat till fluffy. Add egg, sour cream and vanilla. Beat the mixture well.

3. Add dry ingredients to mixture; beat well. (Dough will be sticky.) Cover and chill dough for 2 hours or till it's easy to handle.

4. On a lightly floured surface, roll ⅓ of the dough at a time to ¼-inch thickness. Cut into desired shapes with 2- to 3-inch cookie cutters. Place on ungreased cookie sheets. (If you like, sprinkle with colored sugar now and omit frosting later.)

5. Bake in a 350° oven for about 10 minutes or till edges of cookies are firm and bottoms are golden.

6. Cool cookies on wire racks. If you like, frost cookies with Powdered Sugar Icing and decorate with colored sugar or decorative candies. Makes 60 to 72.

POWDERED SUGAR ICING: In a bowl, mix 2 cups sifted *powdered sugar*, ½ teaspoon *vanilla* and *milk*, 1 tablespoon at a time, till icing is spreadable.

LAUREL'S RAISIN PUFFS

The secret of raisin puffs is to take them from the oven before they get firm, says Laurel West of Concord, Ohio. "They harden as they cool," she promises.

1	cup water
1½	cups raisins
3½	cups all-purpose flour
1	teaspoon baking soda
½	teaspoon salt
1½	cups sugar
1	cup butter, softened
2	eggs
1	teaspoon vanilla
½	cup sugar
1	teaspoon ground cinnamon

1. In a saucepan, boil water. Add raisins; boil till water is gone. Cool. Combine flour, soda and salt. Beat together the 1½ cups sugar and butter till combined. Add eggs and vanilla; beat well. Add dry ingredients to beaten mixture; beat till blended. Stir in raisins.

2. Combine the ½ cup sugar and cinnamon. Shape dough into 1-inch balls; roll in cinnamon sugar. Place 2 inches apart on ungreased cookie sheets. Bake in a 375° oven for 8 minutes. Remove; cool on wire racks. Makes 70.

PEANUT-PRALINE COOKIES

When Tricia Clemans of Valparaiso, Indiana, requests a cookie with "lots of peanuts," her grandmother comes through with these frosted, peanut-packed goodies.

½	cup shortening
½	cup peanut butter
½	cup sugar
½	cup packed brown sugar
1	egg
2	tablespoons milk
1	teaspoon vanilla
1¼	cups all-purpose flour
½	teaspoon baking soda
1½	cups coarsely chopped peanuts
	Praline Frosting

1. Beat shortening and peanut butter till combined. Add sugar and brown sugar; beat till fluffy. Beat in egg, milk and vanilla. Stir in flour and baking soda. Stir in peanuts. If necessary, chill the dough till it's easy to handle.

2. Shape into 1¼-inch balls. Place 2 inches apart on ungreased cookie sheets. Flatten slightly with sugared bottom of a glass. Bake in a 375° oven for 8 to 10 minutes or till set. Cool on wire racks. Drizzle with Praline Frosting. Makes about 40 cookies.

PRALINE FROSTING: In a small saucepan, heat and stir ½ cup packed *brown sugar* and ¼ cup *whipping cream* till bubbly. Reduce heat and simmer for 2 minutes. Remove from heat. Beat in 1 cup sifted *powdered sugar* till smooth.

WIESBADER BROT

The recipe for these crisp cutout cookies comes from one of the original families to settle Iowa's Amana Colonies, that of Marie Reihman, who lived in Middle Amana.

1   cup sugar
½   cup butter or margarine,
        softened
1   egg white
1   egg
2   cups all-purpose flour
1½   teaspoons ground
        cinnamon
1   teaspoon baking powder
1   egg yolk
1   tablespoon milk
2   tablespoons sugar
1   teaspoon ground
        cinnamon

1. Beat together the 1 cup sugar and butter till fluffy. Mix egg white and egg into butter mixture. Combine flour, 1½ teaspoons cinnamon and baking powder. Beat into butter mixture. Cover and chill for at least 3 hours.

2. Roll out half of the dough at a time on a lightly floured surface to ¼-inch thickness. Using cookie cutters, cut into desired shapes. Place cookies 1½ inches apart on ungreased cookie sheets. Stir together reserved egg yolk and milk. Brush on cookies. Combine 2 tablespoons sugar and 1 teaspoon ground cinnamon. Sprinkle on cookies.

3. Bake in a 325° oven for about 10 minutes or till brown. Remove from cookie sheets and cool on wire racks. Makes 40 cookies.

BROOMSTICK COOKIES

Gwen Fox of Somonauk, Illinois, shapes these delicate cookies around a broom handle!

¾   cup finely ground
        unblanched almonds
½   cup unsalted or regular
        butter or margarine
½   cup sugar
2   tablespoons whipping
        cream
1   tablespoon all-purpose
        flour
     Dash salt

1. In a small saucepan, mix all ingredients. Cook and stir over low heat till the butter melts. Drop teaspoonfuls, 4 cookies at a time, 5 inches apart, on a well-buttered and well-floured cookie sheet.

2. Bake in a 350° oven for 4 to 5 minutes or till cookies turn a light golden brown. Remove from oven. Let stand on cookie sheet for 1 to 2 minutes just till cookie edges are firm enough to lift with a spatula. Drape each cookie over a rolling pin or the handle of a broom or wooden spoon. Let cool. Between batches, wipe cookie sheets with a paper towel and re-flour. Makes about 30 cookies.

121

SOUR CREAM TWISTS

"A specialty of my late mother, Edythe Storvick, these cookies are a tasty reminder of my Norwegian heritage," comments Arlene Wee of Huxley, Iowa. We like the flaky, twisted pastry strips warm or cool.

3½ cups all-purpose flour
1 teaspoon salt
1 cup shortening
1 package active dry yeast
¼ cup warm water (105° to 115°)
¾ cup dairy sour cream
1 egg
2 egg yolks
1 teaspoon vanilla
Sugar

1. In mixing bowl, mix flour and salt. Cut in shortening till mixture is size of small peas.

2. Soften yeast in warm water.

3. Combine yeast mixture with sour cream, egg, egg yolks and vanilla. Add all at once to flour mixture. Mix well. Cover and chill for 2 to 3 hours.

4. Divide dough in half. On well-sugared surface, roll half of the dough into 16x8-inch rectangle. Sprinkle with sugar. Fold in edges toward center. Repeat rolling, sprinkling and folding two more times, resugaring surface of dough as needed. Roll to form a 16x8-inch rectangle. Cut lengthwise into two 16x4-inch strips. Cut into thirty-two 4x1-inch strips.

5. Twist and place strips on ungreased cookie sheets, pressing ends down slightly. Repeat rolling, cutting and shaping with second half of cookie dough.

6. Bake in a 375° oven 12 to 15 minutes. Serve warm or cool. Makes 64 cookies.

HUNKA CHOCOLATE COOKIES

This chocolate, butter and nut confection is our version of "the ultimate chocolate cookie."

2 12-ounce packages semisweet chocolate pieces
   (4 cups)
4 squares unsweetened
   chocolate (4 ounces)
¼ cup butter
½ cup all-purpose flour
½ teaspoon baking powder
¼ teaspoon salt
4 eggs
1⅓ cups sugar
2 teaspoons vanilla
2 to 3 cups broken
   walnuts, toasted
   Melted semisweet and
   white chocolate

1. In a heavy saucepan, heat and stir *one package* of semisweet chocolate pieces, unsweetened chocolate and butter till melted. Transfer to large mixing bowl; cool slightly. Stir together flour, baking powder and salt. Set aside.

2. Add eggs, sugar and vanilla to chocolate mixture; beat with an electric mixer. Add flour mixture and beat on low speed till well mixed. Stir in remaining chocolate pieces and nuts. Using ¼ cup dough for each cookie, drop 3 inches apart onto lightly greased cookie sheets. Flatten slightly.

3. Bake in a 350° oven 12 to 15 minutes or till edges are firm and surface is dull and cracked. Let stand 2 minutes. Remove; cool on wire racks. Drizzle with melted semisweet and white chocolate. Makes 24 cookies.

PUMPKIN-NUT COOKIES

We found this recipe in the bake-off winners' file at the Morton, Illinois, pumpkin festival.

2 cups all-purpose flour
4 teaspoons baking powder
1 teaspoon ground
   cinnamon
½ teaspoon salt
¼ teaspoon ground ginger
½ cup shortening
1 cup sugar
2 eggs
1 cup canned pumpkin
1 cup chopped nuts
1 cup raisins
   Orange Icing

1. Stir together flour, baking powder, cinnamon, salt and ginger. Set aside. In a mixing bowl, beat shortening for 30 seconds. Add sugar; beat till fluffy. Beat in eggs and pumpkin. Beat in dry ingredients. Stir in nuts and raisins. Drop by rounded teaspoonfuls onto greased cookie sheets.

2. Bake in a 350° oven for 12 minutes. Remove to wire racks and cool. Drizzle Orange Icing over cookies. Makes 50 cookies.

ORANGE ICING: Mix 1½ cups sifted *powdered sugar*, 1 teaspoon *vanilla* and 2 to 3 tablespoons *orange juice* for drizzle.

JOE CARSON'S GINGER COOKIES

The Silver Dollar City bakery in Branson, Missourri, pulls as many as 40 dozen of these spicy cookies from the oven each day during the Christmas season, says baker Joe Carson.

2 cups all-purpose flour
1 teaspoon baking soda
1 teaspoon ground
   cinnamon
1 teaspoon ground ginger
½ teaspoon ground cloves
½ teaspoon salt
¾ cup shortening
1 cup sugar
2 tablespoons molasses
1 egg

1. Combine flour, baking soda, spices and salt. Beat shortening on medium speed 30 seconds. Add sugar and beat till fluffy. Add molasses and egg. Beat till combined. Add dry ingredients and beat on low speed till well combined.

2. Shape into 1½-inch balls. Dip into a small bowl of *water*, then a bowl of additional sugar. (Or, just dip in sugar.) Arrange 3 inches apart on ungreased cookie sheets. Bake in a 350° oven 15 minutes or till light brown on bottom. Cool on wire racks. Makes 20 cookies.

SWEDISH TEA COOKIES

Tint the filling the color you like in these cookies from Irma Biek of Minocqua, Wisconsin.

1 cup butter or margarine
2 cups all-purpose flour
⅓ cup light cream
   Sugar or colored sugar
¼ cup butter or margarine
2¼ to 2½ cups sifted
   powdered sugar
3 tablespoons milk
1 teaspoon vanilla
   Food coloring

1. Cut 1 cup butter into flour till mixture resembles cornmeal. Stir in cream. On a floured surface, roll dough to ⅛-inch thickness. Cut with 2-inch round cookie cutter.

2. Place on ungreased cookie sheets and sprinkle with sugar. Prick with a fork. Bake in a 375° oven for 8 to 10 minutes or till bottoms are light brown. Remove to wire racks to cool.

3. To prepare the filling, beat ¼ cup butter till fluffy. Gradually beat in *1¼ cups* powdered sugar. Beat in milk and vanilla. Gradually beat in enough of the remaining powdered sugar to make filling spreadable. Tint with food coloring. Spread a small amount of the filling (about a slightly rounded teaspoonful) on the bottom side of half of the cookies, then top with another cookie, sugared side up, to make a sandwich. Makes 36 cookies.

ORANGE SPRITZ COOKIES

Helen Robinson, wife of Pastor Ray E. Robinson at Minocqua, Wisconsin's Church of the Pines, bakes this citrusy version of traditional buttery spritz cookies.

2¼ cups all-purpose flour
1 teaspoon baking powder
¼ teaspoon salt
¾ cup butter or margarine
½ cup sugar
1 egg
2 teaspoons grated orange peel
½ teaspoon almond extract
Colored sugar or decorative candies

1. Stir together the flour, baking powder and salt. Set aside. Beat butter for 30 seconds. Add sugar; beat till fluffy. Beat in egg, orange peel and almond extract. Add dry ingredients and beat till combined. *Do not chill the dough.*

2. Pack dough into a cookie press. Force dough through press onto an ungreased cookie sheet. Decorate with colored sugar or candies.

3. Bake in a 400° oven for 6 to 8 minutes or till done. Remove; cool on racks. Makes 48.

CHOCOLATE BOURBON BALLS

Through the years, Carolyn Crumley's rich chocolate delights have been a big hit in Lee's Summit, Missouri. Bourbon and candied red cherries enhance the holiday treat.

1 6-ounce package semi-sweet chocolate pieces
¼ cup milk
3 tablespoons light corn syrup
2 tablespoons to ¼ cup bourbon
1 9-ounce package chocolate wafers, crushed
1 cup sugar
1 cup finely chopped nuts
½ cup sifted powdered sugar
¼ cup finely chopped candied red cherries
Sifted powdered sugar or unsweetened cocoa powder

1. In a heavy saucepan, heat and stir chocolate over low heat till melted. Stir in milk, corn syrup and bourbon. Set mixture aside.

2. In a large mixing bowl, combine chocolate wafers, the 1 cup sugar, nuts, the ½ cup powdered sugar and the cherries. Add chocolate mixture and stir till combined. Cover and let stand at room temperature for 30 minutes.

3. Shape mixture into 1-inch balls and roll in sugar or cocoa powder. Store in an airtight container at room temperature up to 1 week. Makes 60 balls.

FRENCH PRALINES

Odile Steward Mecker of St. Louis remembers her Grandmother Dodge cooking up batches of these pralines at Christmas. Odile's a descendant of the Pratte and Valle families that were early settlers of Ste. Genevieve, Missouri.

3 cups packed brown sugar
½ cup evaporated milk
1 tablespoon corn syrup
½ cup butter or margarine
3 tablespoons whiskey or brandy
1 tablespoon vinegar
3 cups broken nuts (pecans, black walnuts or hazelnuts)

1. Butter the sides of a heavy, 3-quart saucepan. Add the brown sugar, evaporated milk and corn syrup. Cook and stir over medium-high heat to boiling. Clip on a candy thermometer. Cook and stir over medium-low heat for 5 to 10 minutes to 236° (soft-ball stage). Remove from heat. Add the butter, whiskey or brandy and vinegar. Do not stir. Cool, without stirring, 30 minutes to 150°.

2. Stir in nuts; beat about 5 minutes or till the candy just begins to thicken, but still is glossy. Drop by spoonfuls onto waxed paper. If candy becomes too stiff, stir in a few drops of hot water. Store tightly covered. Makes about 60.

ALMOND BUTTER CRUNCH

Gay Goff of Topeka, Kansas, has the luxury of a generous supply of almonds, thanks to her mother, who owns an almond ranch. Gay and husband Gene capitalize on their nutty annual windfall with almond candy recipes.

1 cup slivered almonds
½ cup butter (not margarine)
½ cup sugar
1 tablespoon light corn syrup

1. Line bottom and sides of a 9-inch round baking pan (do not use a glass pan) with foil. Butter the foil heavily. Set the pan aside.

2. In a 10-inch skillet, combine almonds, butter, sugar and syrup. Cook over medium heat till sugar is melted and mixture turns golden brown, stirring constantly (about 10 minutes).

3. Quickly spread mixture in a pan. Cool for about 15 minutes or till firm.

4. Remove candy by lifting edges of foil. Peel off foil. Cool thoroughly. Makes ¾ pound.

KINGS ISLAND BUCKEYES

From the Kings Island theme park near Cincinnati, Ohio, comes this peanut-butter candy that looks like the nut from Ohio's state tree, the buckeye.

¾ cup butter or margarine
3¼ to 3¾ cups sifted
   powdered sugar
1 cup peanut butter
2 tablespoons whipping
   cream or 1 tablespoon
   milk
½ teaspoon vanilla
16 ounces chocolate-
   flavored candy
   coating, cut up

1. Melt butter over low heat. In a mixing bowl, combine the melted butter with *2 cups* of the powdered sugar. Beat till smooth. Beat in peanut butter till mixed. Stir in cream and vanilla. Continue beating in enough of the remaining powdered sugar till mixture is firm. (Mixture will look crumbly.) Roll into 1-inch balls. Arrange on a tray; chill for 30 minutes.

2. Meanwhile, in a heavy saucepan, melt the candy coating over low heat for dipping. Set aside to cool slightly. Using a fork, dip each ball into melted candy coating so it covers ¾ of each ball to resemble a buckeye. (If the chocolate dipping mixture hardens, remelt over low heat.) Place undipped side up on a waxed-paper-lined tray. Chill till firm. Store in refrigerator. Makes about 72.

TORTUGAS

These tortoise-shaped candies come from Elaine Gonzalez of Northbrook, Illinois.

24 caramels
¾ pound white chocolate,
   melted and tempered,
   or confectioner's
   coating, melted
72 jumbo roasted cashews

1. Unwrap caramels. Place in bowl over *warm water* 15 minutes to soften. Meanwhile, on a baking sheet lined with waxed paper, spoon dollops (about 1 teaspoon) of white chocolate 2 inches apart. Place 2 cashews (on their sides) on each dollop of chocolate to form feet.

2. Roll softened caramels to form ¾-inch balls. Flatten slightly. Place on cashews to form tortoise shells. Spoon additional melted white chocolate over the caramel to coat the shells. Stick a cashew, narrow end down, against the coated shell to form a tortoise head. Chill till set. Makes 24.

OLD-FASHIONED BONBONS

Step back in time to Christmas past with a holiday-season visit to Conner Prairie in Noblesville, Indiana. Chat with villagers re-enacting Christmas Eve in 1836 as you stroll along candlelit paths. Then, stop in at the Festival of Gingerbread, an exhibit of 100 gingerbread houses. Here's a typical holiday candy one of the villagers might be making.

1½ cups sugar
1½ cups packed brown sugar
1 5-ounce can evaporated milk (⅔ cup)
1 tablespoon butter or margarine
1 teaspoon vanilla
1 pound chocolate-flavored or white candy coating, melted and cooled slightly
   Finely chopped nuts, coconut or decorative candies (optional)

1. Butter the sides of a heavy, 2-quart saucepan. In the saucepan, combine the sugars and milk. Cook and stir over medium-high heat to boiling, stirring constantly with a wooden spoon to dissolve sugar (should take about 8 minutes). Carefully clip candy thermometer to side of pan. Cook and stir over medium-low heat 3 to 4 minutes or to 234° (soft-ball stage), stirring frequently.

2. Remove saucepan from heat. Add butter or margarine and vanilla, but don't stir. Without stirring, cool to 150° (35 minutes). Remove thermometer.

3. Beat mixture vigorously till candy thickens and loses its gloss. Then, knead till firm. (If necessary, cool mixture slightly till easy to handle.) Divide into quarters. Shape each quarter into a 1-inch-wide rope about 12 inches long. Cut into ¾-inch pieces and shape each piece into a ball. Meanwhile, keep remaining quarters tightly wrapped in plastic wrap. Repeat with remaining quarters.

4. Dip candy pieces in melted confectioner's coating; let excess coating or chocolate drip off candy. Place dipped candy on a baking sheet lined with waxed paper.

5. If you like, sprinkle with nuts, coconut or decorative candies. Let stand till chocolate is dry. Makes 64 bonbons.

DESSERTS

Raspberry Freeze

Peach-Almond
Sauce

Caramel-Pecan
Ice Cream

DESSERTS

OLD-FASHIONED STRAWBERRY SHORTCAKE

Representatives of the Trojan Senior Citizens Center prepare this crowd pleaser for Troy, Ohio's Strawberry Festival. They bake the cakes ahead to fill with berries they handpick.

6 cups stemmed fresh strawberries (3 pints)
½ cup sugar
1 cup whipping cream
2 tablespoons powdered sugar
2 cups all-purpose flour
¼ cup sugar
1 tablespoon baking powder
½ teaspoon salt
½ teaspoon ground nutmeg (optional)
½ cup butter or margarine
1 egg
⅔ cup milk
2 tablespoons butter or margarine, melted

1. Set aside a few strawberries for garnishing. Crush *half* of the remaining berries with a fork. Slice remaining berries and stir into crushed berries with ½ cup sugar. Set aside.

2. Beat whipping cream and powdered sugar till stiff peaks form. Cover and chill.

3. Stir together the flour, ¼ cup sugar, baking powder, salt and nutmeg, if you like. Cut in the ½ cup butter or margarine till the mixture resembles coarse crumbs.

4. In another bowl, beat together the egg and milk. Add to the flour mixture and mix till just moistened. Spread mixture evenly into a greased 9x1½-inch round baking pan. Bake in a 425° oven for 18 to 20 minutes or till golden. Loosen the edge with a knife and remove shortcake from pan.

5. Cool the baked shortcake for 15 minutes. Slit the cake into 2 layers and lift the top off carefully. Brush the cut side of the bottom layer of the shortcake with the melted butter or margarine. Spoon half of the strawberry-sugar mixture on top of that layer.

6. Place the top of the shortcake on the strawberry-sugar mixture and spoon on the remaining strawberries and sugar. Mound whipped cream on top and garnish with strawberries. Serve the filled shortcake warm and cut into wedges. Pass the remaining whipped cream. Makes 8 servings.

STRAWBERRY NESTS

In this easy dessert, wine and a cream-yogurt sauce complement ruby-red strawberries from New Prague, Minnesota, or hundreds of other berry-growing areas in the Midwest.

1 pint strawberries, halved
¼ cup sifted powdered sugar
¼ cup sweet Marsala, ruby port or brandy
½ cup whipping cream
½ cup vanilla yogurt
2 tablespoons powdered sugar
¼ teaspoon ground nutmeg or mace

1. Toss strawberries with the ¼ cup powdered sugar and Marsala. Cover; chill 2 to 6 hours.

2. Thirty minutes or less before serving, in a chilled bowl, combine whipping cream, yogurt, 2 tablespoons of the powdered sugar and nutmeg. Beat till fluffy. Cover and chill up to 30 minutes.

3. Spoon berries and juice into 4 serving dishes, forming nests. Spoon whipped mixture in center. Makes 4 servings.

CANTALOUPE SHORTCAKE

Melon fans from southern Indiana recommend cantaloupe instead of berries on shortcake.

2 cups all-purpose flour
2 tablespoons sugar
1 tablespoon baking powder
¼ teaspoon ground nutmeg
½ cup butter or margarine
1 beaten egg
⅔ cup milk
1 tablespoon sugar
  Dash ground nutmeg
  Dash ground cinnamon
2 cups peeled, seeded and coarsely chopped cantaloupe
1 cup fresh or frozen blueberries, partially thawed
¼ cup sugar
1 cup whipping cream
2 tablespoons sugar

1. Mix flour, 2 tablespoons sugar, baking powder, ¼ teaspoon nutmeg and ⅛ teaspoon *salt*. Cut in butter till mixture resembles coarse crumbs. Combine egg and milk; add all at once to flour mixture. Stir till just moistened.

2. In a greased 8x1½-inch round baking pan, spread dough, building up edges slightly. Stir together 1 tablespoon sugar, dash nutmeg and cinnamon; sprinkle over dough in pan. Bake in a 450° oven for 15 to 18 minutes. Cool in pan for 15 minutes; remove to serving plate.

3. Toss together cantaloupe, blueberries and ¼ cup sugar. Whip cream with 2 tablespoons sugar till stiff peaks form (tips stand straight).

4. To assemble, split cake into 2 layers while warm; carefully lift off the top layer. Alternate layers of cake, fruit and whipped cream. Serve warm. Makes 8 servings.

VERY BERRY SURPRISE

At the Old Church Inn in St. Charles, Illinois, diners often choose this fruity dessert.

2 cups frozen unsweetened loose-pack raspberries
1½ cups frozen unsweetened loose-pack strawberries
1 6-ounce package raspberry-flavored gelatin
½ cup dairy sour cream
2 tablespoons lemon juice
1 pint strawberry or vanilla ice cream
   Whipped cream
   Maraschino cherries

1. Thaw berries, but do not drain. Place berries and juice in blender container. Cover; blend till pureed. Sieve into mixing bowl, discarding seeds.

2. Stir the gelatin into 1 cup *boiling water* till gelatin dissolves. Transfer to the blender container. Add sour cream, lemon juice and ice cream to blender. Cover; blend smooth. Stir into berries. Pour into serving bowl or dishes. Cover; chill 4 to 6 hours to firm. Serve topped with cream and cherries. Serves 8 to 10.

STRAWBERRY-COOKIE PIZZA

This is a large version of the individual dessert pizzas the Ladies' Auxiliary Miami No. 971 (Fraternal Order of Eagles) serves at Troy, Ohio's Strawberry Festival.

½ of a 20-ounce roll refrigerated sugar-cookie dough
2 3-ounce packages cream cheese, softened
2 tablespoons sugar
2 tablespoons orange juice
1 small banana
1½ cups sliced strawberries
¼ to ½ cup drained pineapple tidbits
¼ cup strawberry jelly or jam

1. Cut cookie dough into ½-inch-thick slices. Arrange the slices on an ungreased cookie sheet to form an 8-inch circle. Bake the cookie crust in a 400° oven for about 12 minutes or till the crust is done. Cool for 5 minutes on the cookie sheet. Using a spatula, loosen edges of the crust and transfer to a wire rack to cool.

2. Beat the cream cheese, sugar and 2 tablespoons *orange juice* with an electric mixer till fluffy. Spread over the cooled crust.

3. Thinly bias-slice the banana. Brush with additional *orange juice.* Arrange evenly over crust with the strawberries and the pineapple.

4. Heat the jelly or jam over low heat till melted. Drizzle over the pizza. Cut pizza into wedges to serve. Store any remaining pizza, covered, in the refrigerator. Makes 6 servings.

PEACHY OZARK COBBLER

Credit this recipe to an old-time cookbook from Silver Dollar City, the theme park at Branson, Missouri. Some Ozark cooks substitute raspberries for peaches in this eye-catching dessert that's pictured on the cover.

3 cups cake flour
1 teaspoon salt
1 cup lard or shortening
⅓ to ½ cup ice-cold water
7 cups peeled, thinly sliced fresh peaches or frozen, unsweetened peach slices, thawed
¾ cup sugar
2 tablespoons all-purpose flour
¼ teaspoon ground nutmeg
3 tablespoons butter or margarine
Melted butter or margarine
Sugar
Ground nutmeg
Ozark Dip

1. Combine cake flour and salt. Cut in lard till mixture resembles coarse crumbs. Gradually pour in water; blend to form pastry dough. Divide into 2 portions of ⅓ and ⅔.

2. On waxed paper, pat or roll larger portion of pastry into a 12x12-inch square. Fit into bottom and up sides of 2-quart square baking dish. Trim pastry.

3. Toss peaches with ¾ cup sugar, flour and ¼ teaspoon nutmeg; spoon into dish. Dot with 3 tablespoons butter or margarine.

4. Roll remaining pastry into a 9x7-inch rectangle. Cut into 1-inch-wide strips. Arrange pastry strips over peaches; trim to fit dish. Brush with melted butter or margarine. Sprinkle with some sugar and nutmeg.

5. Bake in a 375° oven for 55 to 60 minutes or till pastry browns. Pour Ozark Dip over servings. Makes 8 to 10 servings.

OZARK DIP: Mix 1 cup *milk*, 1 teaspoon *sugar* and dash ground *nutmeg*.

CARAMEL-APPLE PANDOWDY

"It's like an apple pie with apple cake on top," says Victorian Villa innkeeper Ron Gibson. He serves this warm with cream at his Union City, Michigan, inn.

5   McIntosh or Golden
    Delicious apples
5   Granny Smith or Pippin
    apples
1½ cups packed brown sugar
1   cup butter or margarine
2   cups all-purpose flour
1   tablespoon baking
    powder
¼   teaspoon *each* ground
    cinnamon, ground
    nutmeg and allspice
1   cup sugar
2   eggs
1   cup applesauce
½   cup raisins
½   cup chopped pecans

1. Peel, core and thinly slice apples. (You should have 5 cups of each type.) In greased 3-quart rectangular baking dish, place apples. Top with brown sugar. Dot with *½ cup* butter.

2. Stir together flour, baking powder, spices and ¼ teaspoon *salt*. Beat the remaining ½ cup butter for 1 minute. Beat in sugar, then eggs.

3. Add dry ingredients and applesauce alternately to beaten mixture, beating well. Stir in raisins and pecans.

4. Spoon the batter evenly over the apples. Bake in 350° oven for 45 to 50 minutes or till the cake tests done. Serve warm with *cream,* if you like. Makes 12 to 16 servings.

CARAMEL APPLE-NUT SQUARES

This dessert comes from the Harvest Baking Contest in New Albany, Indiana.

1¾ cups all-purpose flour
1   cup quick-cooking oats
½   cup packed brown sugar
½   teaspoon baking soda
½   teaspoon salt
1   cup butter or margarine
20 caramels, unwrapped
1   14-ounce can sweetened
    condensed milk
1   21-ounce can apple pie
    filling
1   cup chopped walnuts
    Cinnamon or vanilla ice
    cream

1. For crust, mix flour, oats, brown sugar, baking soda and salt. Cut in butter till crumbly. Reserve *1 cup* of the mixture. Press remaining mixture into 13x9x2-inch baking pan. Bake the crust layer in a 375° oven for 10 minutes.

2. For filling, in heavy saucepan, melt caramels with condensed milk over low heat, stirring till smooth. Spoon pie filling over crust. Top with caramel mixture. Sprinkle reserved crumb mixture over caramel layer. Top with nuts.

3. Return to oven and bake for about 20 minutes more or till top is golden. Cool on wire rack. Serve with ice cream. Serves 15 to 20.

RHUBARB-ALMOND COBBLER

When rhubarb comes up in Iowa in mid-May, the occasion calls for this luscious dessert.

1   cup sugar
½   cup water
6   cups fresh rhubarb, cut
        into ½-inch pieces, or
        frozen sliced rhubarb
2   tablespoons all-purpose
        flour
2   tablespoons butter or
        margarine
½   cup toasted slivered
        almonds or pecans
1   cup all-purpose flour
2   tablespoons sugar
1½   teaspoons baking powder
¼   cup butter or margarine
1   slightly beaten egg
¼   cup milk

1. In large saucepan, mix *½ cup* of the sugar and water. Bring to boil; add rhubarb. Reduce heat. Cover and simmer 5 minutes or till tender. Mix remaining ½ cup sugar and 2 tablespoons flour. Add to rhubarb mixture. Cook and stir till thickened and bubbly. Stir in 2 tablespoons butter and nuts. Keep hot.

2. For topper, mix 1 cup flour, 2 tablespoons sugar, baking powder and ¼ teaspoon *salt*. Cut in the ¼ cup butter till mixture resembles coarse crumbs. Mix egg and milk; add all at once to dry ingredients; stir just to moisten.

3. Turn hot rhubarb into a 1½-quart round casserole. Quickly spoon topper in 6 mounds atop. Bake in a 400° oven for about 20 minutes or till golden. Serve warm. Serves 6.

NECTARINE-RASPBERRY CRISP

Judie and Bob Weil of St. Louis Park, Minnesota, take advantage of summer's bounty of fruits for this recipe. If you can't get nectarines, substitute peaches.

2   large nectarines
⅓   cup apricot preserves
1   teaspoon vanilla
2   cups fresh raspberries
½   cup all-purpose flour
⅓   cup packed brown sugar
½   teaspoon ground
        cinnamon
¼   teaspoon ground nutmeg
⅓   cup butter or margarine
1   cup granola
¼   cup toasted slivered
        almonds, chopped
     Vanilla ice cream

1. Halve, pit and cut nectarines into ½-inch slices. In an 8x1½-inch round baking pan, stir together nectarines, preserves and vanilla. Carefully fold in berries.

2. In a bowl, combine flour, sugar, cinnamon and nutmeg. Cut in butter till mixture resembles coarse crumbs. Add granola and almonds. Toss with a fork till mixed. Sprinkle the mixture over the fruit in baking pan.

3. Bake in a 375° oven for 25 to 30 minutes or till topping is golden. Serve warm or at room temperature with ice cream. Makes 6 servings.

JUMBO APPLE DUMPLINGS

Nadine Shirley, one of the volunteers known as Apple Pandowdies at the Apple Jubilee in Waverly, Missouri, passed away a few years ago. But her daughter, Pat Maycock, continues Nadine's tradition of baking apple dumplings for the celebration.

2 cups all-purpose flour
2 teaspoons baking powder
1 teaspoon salt
⅔ cup shortening
⅓ to ½ cup milk
6 medium cooking apples, peeled and cored (about 5 ounces each)
1 cup sugar
1¼ teaspoons ground cinnamon
2 tablespoons butter or margarine
1½ cups sugar
1½ cups water
¼ teaspoon ground cinnamon
¼ teaspoon ground nutmeg
3 tablespoons butter or margarine
Ice cream or cream

1. In a mixing bowl, combine the flour, baking powder and salt. Using a pastry blender, cut in the shortening till it's about the size of small peas. Sprinkle *1 tablespoon* of the milk over a part of the mixture; gently toss with a fork. Push to side of bowl. Repeat till all is moistened. Divide into 6 equal portions. Form each into a ball. Cover and set aside.

2. On a lightly floured surface, roll out each portion of dough into a 7½- to 8-inch circle, trimming uneven edges. Place an apple in the center of each circle of dough.

3. Combine the 1 cup sugar and 1¼ teaspoons cinnamon. Divide the mixture among the apples, sprinkling it into the center. Top each with some of the 2 tablespoons butter.

4. Moisten the edge of pastry with some *water*. Bring dough up around each apple to resemble a bundle, pressing the edges together at the top to seal. Cut any remaining dough into decorative leaf shapes to place on top of the apples. Arrange in a lightly greased 3-quart rectangular baking dish.

5. For syrup, in a saucepan, combine 1½ cups sugar, 1½ cups water, ¼ teaspoon cinnamon and nutmeg. Bring to boiling. Remove from heat and stir in 3 tablespoons butter. Pour over apples in the baking dish.

6. Bake in a 375° oven for 35 to 40 minutes or till done. Serve warm with ice cream or cream. Makes 6 servings.

THE SLUICE'S BREAD PUDDING WITH CARAMEL SAUCE

At this Spearfish, South Dakota, restaurant, they ladle warm Caramel Sauce over this old-fashioned dessert. The bread pudding is equally delicious served warm or chilled.

1 1-pound loaf Vienna bread
6 eggs
3½ cups milk
1½ cups sugar
1 cup light cream
2 teaspoons vanilla
½ cup raisins
   Caramel Sauce

1. Cut the bread into 1-inch cubes. Spread bread cubes in a shallow baking pan, cover loosely and let dry overnight.

2. In a mixing bowl, beat together the eggs, milk, sugar, cream and vanilla.

3. In a very large mixing bowl, combine the bread cubes and raisins. Pour milk mixture over bread and raisins. Stir till bread is soaked with milk mixture.

4. Turn mixture into a well-buttered 13x9x2-inch baking pan. Cover with foil. Bake in a 325° oven for about 1 hour or till set.

5. Prepare Caramel Sauce.

6. Top warm or cold bread pudding with warm sauce. Makes 12 servings.

CARAMEL SAUCE: In a heavy, medium saucepan, combine ½ cup *butter* or *margarine,* ½ cup *sugar,* ½ cup packed *brown sugar* and ½ cup *whipping cream.* Cook and stir over medium-high heat till mixture boils. Stir in 1 teaspoon *vanilla.* Serve sauce immediately over bread pudding or cool, cover and store sauce in the refrigerator for up to 7 days. Warm in microwave oven (see below) or in a saucepan before serving. Makes 1¾ cups.

Note: To reheat sauce in microwave oven, place sauce in 4-cup glass measure and cook on 100% power (high) for 1 to 1½ minutes.

CRANBERRY PUDDING WITH VANILLA SAUCE

Fielding E. Utz of Grafton, Wisconsin (the Heartland's cranberry state), salvaged his grandmother's treasured pudding recipe, as well as the steamer she made it in. Now, he carries on the family's yuletide tradition when he serves the dessert. He complements the cranberry-molasses flavor with a sweet sauce—as his grandmother did.

1½   cups all-purpose flour
1   teaspoon baking soda
¼   teaspoon salt
½   cup light molasses
½   cup boiling water
1   teaspoon vanilla
2   cups coarsely chopped
        cranberries
     Creamy Vanilla Sauce

1. In a bowl, stir together flour, baking soda and salt. Set aside.

2. In a medium mixing bowl, combine the molasses, water and vanilla. Stir in the dry ingredients till just combined. Fold in the cranberries. Pour the pudding mixture into a greased and floured 4-cup mold or 1-quart round casserole. Cover with foil.

3. Place the mold or casserole on a wire rack in a deep kettle; add boiling water to the kettle to the depth of 1 inch. Cover the kettle and steam the pudding for 2 to 2¼ hours or till a toothpick inserted near the center of the pudding comes out clean. (Add more water as needed during cooking.)

4. Cool the cooked pudding on a wire rack for 10 minutes, then unmold. Prepare Creamy Vanilla Sauce. Serve the pudding warm with the sauce. Makes 6 to 8 servings.

CREAMY VANILLA SAUCE: In a small bowl, stir together 1 cup *sugar* and 1 teaspoon *all-purpose flour;* set aside. In a small saucepan, melt ½ cup *butter* or *margarine.* Stir in ½ cup *whipping cream* and ½ teaspoon *vanilla.* Add the sugar mixture and cook over medium heat till the sugar is dissolved. Serve the sauce warm over the warm pudding. Makes 1½ cups.

RHUBARB-STRAWBERRY SORBET

Rhubarb is one of the earliest spring crops all across the Midwest. Cooks everywhere pride themselves on creating delicious rhubarb recipes like this refreshing dessert.

1   cup sugar
½   cup water
4   cups fresh rhubarb cut into ½-inch pieces or one 16-ounce package frozen unsweetened sliced rhubarb
½   cup strawberry liqueur or raspberry liqueur
   Sliced pears, honeydew, peaches or kiwifruit (optional)

1. In large saucepan, heat sugar and water till sugar dissolves. Add rhubarb. Bring to boiling; reduce heat. Cover and simmer for 5 minutes or till rhubarb is tender.

2. Transfer half of the rhubarb mixture to blender container or food processor bowl and blend or process till smooth. Pour into a large bowl. Repeat for remaining rhubarb. Cool; chill thoroughly, about 2 hours.

3. Stir strawberry or raspberry liqueur into rhubarb mixture. Pour mixture into ice cream freezer container. Freeze according to manufacturer's directions. Serve sorbet by itself or with fruit, if you like. Makes 1 quart.

MAPLE FRANGO

In the Midwest's maple-syrup country, folks sweeten just about everything with maple syrup. This frozen delight is ice-cream smooth and delicious—worth every calorie!

¾   cup pure maple syrup
3   egg yolks
1   cup whipping cream

1. In a small, heavy saucepan, heat maple syrup till just boiling.

2. Meanwhile, in a small bowl, beat egg yolks. Gradually stir about half of the hot syrup into the beaten yolks; return all to saucepan. Cook and stir over medium heat till bubbly. Cook and stir 2 minutes more. Cool thoroughly.

3. Beat whipping cream till soft peaks form. Fold into maple mixture. Pour into an 8x8x2-inch pan. Cover with foil. Freeze for 2 to 3 hours without stirring till the consistency of soft-serve ice cream. Makes 4 servings.

CHOCOLATE-PEANUT BUTTER ICE CREAM

The ice cream social is a Midwest institution. This recipe and the one below are just two examples of the cool and creamy concoctions you'll find at these summer gatherings.

2   cups light cream
1   16-ounce can chocolate fudge ice cream topping
1   tablespoon vanilla
1   cup chopped chocolate-covered peanut butter cups (about 6½ ounces)

1. In ice cream container, stir together cream, chocolate ice cream topping and vanilla. (Topping won't blend well with stirring, but will during the freezing process.) Freeze according to manufacturer's directions.

2. Remove dasher. Gently stir chopped candy into ice cream. Cover; let ripen in freezer. Makes about 1½ quarts.

CARAMEL-PECAN ICE CREAM

Expect a crunch with every spoonful of this irresistible summertime treat.

2   cups light cream
1   12-ounce jar caramel ice cream topping
½   cup packed brown sugar
1½ teaspoons vanilla
2   cups whipping cream
⅔   cup Pecan Clusters, broken into small pieces

1. In a large bowl, combine light cream, caramel topping, brown sugar and vanilla. Stir till the sugar is dissolved. Stir in the whipping cream and Pecan Clusters.

2. Pour mixture into a 2-quart (or larger) ice cream freezer container. Freeze cream mixture according to manufacturer's directions.

3. Remove dasher. Cover; let ripen in freezer. Makes about 1½ quarts.

PECAN CLUSTERS: In a heavy 8-inch skillet, combine 1 cup coarsely chopped *pecans*, ½ cup *sugar* and 2 tablespoons *butter* or *margarine*. Heat over medium heat, stirring constantly, for 6 to 8 minutes or till sugar melts and turns a rich brown color. Remove from heat. Drop candied nuts in clusters onto a buttered baking sheet or foil. Cool.

RASPBERRY FREEZE
When the heat of summer gets to be too much, folks in the Midwest break for a dip or two of their favorite sherbet or ice cream—ones like this freeze and the ice cream below.

- 3 beaten eggs
- 2 cups light cream
- 1 cup sugar
- 1 cup whipping cream
- ½ teaspoon vanilla
- 3 cups fresh red raspberries or frozen unsweetened raspberries

1. In saucepan, combine eggs, light cream and sugar. Cook and stir over medium heat till slightly thickened and the mixture coats a metal spoon. Cool; chill.

2. In ice cream container, combine egg mixture, whipping cream, vanilla and fresh or frozen raspberries. Freeze according to manufacturer's directions. Makes 1½ quarts.

MARSHMALLOW ICE CREAM
No cranking! Make this ice cream in a pan in your freezer. It's a smooth, snow-white treat perfect for a fresh fruit topping, like our Strawberry-Coconut Sauce (recipe, page 144).

- 2 cups milk
- 3 cups miniature marshmallows
- ⅔ cup sugar
- 2 8-ounce cartons dairy sour cream
- 2 teaspoons vanilla

1. In a 3-quart saucepan, heat milk, marshmallows and sugar till marshmallows are melted and sugar is dissolved. Cool. Stir in sour cream and vanilla. Turn into an 8x8x2-inch baking pan. Cover; freeze till partially frozen.

2. Break frozen mixture into chunks. Turn into a chilled large mixer bowl. Beat with electric mixer just till fluffy. Return to cold pan. Cover; freeze till firm. Makes about 1 quart.

CHAMPAGNE FRUIT BOWL
Champagne adds sparkle to this favorite of Marilyn Schudy of Kansas City, Missouri.

- 1 quart strawberries
- 2 oranges
- 2 kiwifruit
- 1½ cups seedless red or green grapes
- 2 to 3 tablespoons sugar
- 1½ cups champagne

1. Halve strawberries. Peel and section oranges. Peel and slice kiwifruit. In a large bowl, combine fruit and sugar. Cover and chill till serving time.

2. Just before serving, pour champagne over fruit in bowl. Serve with a slotted spoon. Makes 8 to 10 servings.

PEACH-ALMOND SAUCE

Because recipes for sauces from Heartland soda fountains usually are top secret, we've developed this sauce and the one below for you to try.

3   cups peeled fresh peach slices
¼   cup toasted slivered almonds
⅓   cup sugar
3   tablespoons Amaretto
1½ teaspoons lemon juice

1. In a bowl, combine peaches and almonds. In a small bowl, stir together sugar, Amaretto and lemon juice. Pour over peaches. Cover the surface with clear plastic wrap, pressing out air bubbles to prevent peaches from browning. Chill for up to 4 hours. Serve over ice cream or other desserts. Makes 2 cups of topping.

HOT-FUDGE SAUCE

Rich, creamy, delicious—everything a homemade hot-fudge sauce should be.

5   squares (5 ounces) semi-sweet chocolate, cut up
½   cup whipping cream
¼   cup sugar
1   teaspoon vanilla

1. In a small, heavy saucepan, combine chocolate, cream and sugar. Cook and stir over low heat till chocolate melts and sauce becomes smooth. Stir in vanilla. Serve warm. Store any remaining sauce in tightly covered container in refrigerator. Reheat to serve. Makes 1 cup.

A HONEY OF A PLUM SAUCE

Iowa garden writer Jan Riggenbach transforms fresh plums into a honey-flavored sauce to serve warm or cold over ice cream and other treats.

1   cup honey
½   cup pineapple juice
½   teaspoon ground cinnamon
4   cups pitted and chopped fresh plums (about 1½ pounds fresh plums)

1. In a large saucepan, combine the honey, pineapple juice and ground cinnamon. Cook and stir the mixture till it's bubbly. Add the pitted and chopped plums. Return to boiling. Boil gently about 10 minutes or till the plum mixture is slightly thickened and syrupy, stirring occasionally. (The cooking time will vary, depending on the type of plums you use.)

2. Serve the sauce warm or cold over ice cream. Or you can ladle the sauce into freezer containers. Cover, seal, label and freeze. Makes 3 cups of plum sauce.

STRAWBERRY-COCONUT SAUCE

In berry patches across the Midwest, grow the firm ripe strawberries that give recipes, like this topping, their unique flavor twist.

1 cup sliced fresh
   strawberries
   Orange juice
2 teaspoons cornstarch
½ cup currant jelly or
   strawberry jelly
2 cups sliced fresh
   strawberries
¼ cup toasted coconut

1. In a blender container, blend the 1 cup of strawberries till they're pureed. Add enough orange juice to pureed strawberries to measure 1 cup. Stir in cornstarch; mix well.

2. In a saucepan, heat jelly over medium heat till just melted. Stir in pureed strawberry mixture. Cook and stir the mixture till thickened and bubbly. Cook and stir 1 to 2 minutes more. Cool; chill thoroughly, about 4 hours.

3. Just before serving, fold 2 cups of fresh strawberries and toasted coconut into strawberry sauce. Serve as a topping for ice cream or other desserts. Makes about 3 cups topping.

RASPBERRY-ORANGE SAUCE

Citrus and Midwest-grown raspberries blend for a flavorful dessert sauce that's ready in 10 minutes in your microwave oven.

½ teaspoon finely shredded
   orange peel
¾ cup orange juice
¼ cup sugar
1 tablespoon cornstarch
2 cups fresh raspberries or
   2 cups loose-pack
   frozen red raspberries,
   black raspberries or
   blackberries

1. In a microwave-safe 4-cup measuring cup, combine the finely shredded orange peel with the orange juice, sugar and the cornstarch.

2. Microcook the juice mixture, uncovered, on 100% power (high) for 2 to 3 minutes or till thickened and bubbly, stirring every minute till slightly thickened, then stirring the juice mixture every 30 seconds.

3. Stir in berries. Microcook for 1 to 3 minutes more or till mixture is heated through. Serve warm over unfrosted cake, bread pudding or ice cream. Makes about 2 cups sauce.

Note: Chill any leftover sauce and serve cold or reheat it.

DOLCE AL CAFFEE

This coffee-flavored Italian dessert is a specialty of Rina Fontanini of Highland Park, Illinois.

1   pound butter or
       margarine
2   cups sugar
⅓   cup refrigerated or frozen
       egg product
1   cup prepared instant or
       brewed espresso coffee
2½ 3-ounce packages
       ladyfingers (about 30)
       Anisette liqueur
1   cup whipping cream,
       whipped

1. In mixer bowl, beat butter 30 seconds. Add sugar; beat till combined. Add egg product alternately with coffee till well blended (mixture will resemble frosting). Set aside.

2. Sprinkle ladyfingers with some Anisette just to moisten. Arrange in 2-quart bowl or 8- or 9-inch springform pan to cover bottom and sides. Layer cream mixture and remaining ladyfingers in bowl or pan, starting with cream mixture and finishing with ladyfingers. (You'll have 4 to 6 layers, depending on how deep the bowl is.) Cover and chill for 4 to 24 hours.

3. To serve, unmold from bowl onto a serving plate or remove sides from springform pan. Cover or top with whipped cream. Slice to serve. Refrigerate remaining cake. Serves 12.

ZINGERMAN'S NOODLE KUGEL

Jewish cooks have been using their noodles for years to make this dish, which you can eat either as a side dish or for dessert— as diners do at the famous Ann Arbor, Michigan, deli.

6   ounces packaged
       fettuccine
1½ cups shredded farmer's
       cheese (6 ounces)
1   cup raisins
1   8-ounce container dairy
       sour cream
⅓   cup sugar
1   teaspoon vanilla
½   teaspoon ground
       cinnamon
¼   teaspoon salt
5   beaten eggs

1. In a large saucepan, cook fettuccine according to package directions till just tender. Drain and rinse under cold water. Drain; set aside.

2. In a large bowl, stir together cheese, raisins, sour cream, sugar, vanilla, cinnamon and salt.

3. Stir in the eggs. Fold in fettuccine.

4. Turn mixture into a buttered 2-quart square baking dish. Pat noodles down so they're covered with egg mixture.

5. Bake in a 325° oven for 30 to 35 minutes or till edges begin to brown. Makes 8 servings.

INDIANA APPLE CAKE ROLL

This unique dessert is a specialty of Tony Hanslits of Square I Grill in Indianapolis.

⅓ cup sifted cake flour
3 tablespoons cornstarch
1 teaspoon ground
  cinnamon
2 egg yolks
2 eggs
¾ teaspoon vanilla
½ cup sugar
2 egg whites
¼ teaspoon cream of tartar
¼ cup sugar
  Sifted powdered sugar
¼ cup water
2 tablespoon sugar
1 teaspoon ground
  cinnamon
1 cup apple butter
1 cup peeled, finely
  chopped Granny
  Smith apples or other
  tart, crisp apples
  Wine Custard (see recipe,
  page 147)

1. For cake roll, mix first 3 ingredients. Set aside. In large mixing bowl, mix yolks, eggs and vanilla. Beat with electric mixer on high speed for 5 minutes or till thick. Gradually add ½ cup sugar; beat till dissolved. Sprinkle half of the flour mixture over yolk mixture; fold in gently. Repeat with remaining flour.

2. Wash beaters. Beat whites and cream of tartar till soft peaks form (tips curl). Gradually add ¼ cup sugar, beating till stiff peaks form (tips stand straight). Fold into yolk mixture.

3. Spread batter evenly into a greased and floured 15x10x1-inch jelly-roll pan. Bake in a 375° oven for 12 to 15 minutes or till cake springs back when lightly touched near center. Immediately loosen sides from pan and turn out onto a towel sprinkled with powdered sugar. Roll up towel and cake, jelly-roll style, starting from one of the short sides. Let stand 10 minutes. Gently unroll; cover till cooled.

4. To prepare syrup, combine the ¼ cup water, 2 tablespoons sugar and 1 teaspoon cinnamon. Bring to boiling, stirring till sugar dissolves. Remove from heat; let cool. To prepare the filling, in saucepan, mix apple butter and apples. Bring to boiling. Reduce heat. Simmer, uncovered, for 5 to 8 minutes or till apples are tender. Remove from heat; cool.

5. To assemble, sprinkle inside of cake with syrup. Spread with filling and roll up. Wrap in clear plastic wrap; chill at least 3 hours.

6. Unwrap; sprinkle with powdered sugar. Slice; serve with Wine Custard. Serves 10.

WINE CUSTARD

To serve the Indiana Apple Cake Roll on page 146, spoon some of this stirred custard onto individual plates and lay cake slices on the custard.

6   egg yolks
1   cup Reisling wine or
      other white wine
½   cup sugar
1   cup whipping cream

1. In the top of a double boiler, beat egg yolks and wine till combined. Stir in sugar. Place over *boiling water* (water shouldn't touch upper pan). Whisk by hand or beat with an electric mixer on high speed about 10 minutes or till custard mixture thickens.

2. When thick, place the pan over *ice water* (if using a glass pan, transfer the mixture to a metal bowl). Continue beating 2 to 3 minutes or till cool. Beat in whipping cream till soft peaks form. Fold into custard. Cover and chill 3 to 24 hours. Stir before serving.

CHERRY-NUT APPLESAUCE

The dried cherries used in this unique applesauce are a favorite in Michigan and other parts of the Midwest. Use your microwave oven to cook this applesauce in a flash.

½   cup sugar
⅓   cup orange juice
½   teaspoon ground
      cinnamon
¼   teaspoon ground allspice
6   medium baking apples
      (about 2 pounds),
      peeled, quartered
      and cored
¼   cup snipped dried
      cherries or raisins
2   tablespoons chopped
      walnuts

1. In a microwave-safe 2-quart casserole, mix the sugar, orange juice, cinnamon and allspice.

2. Add the apples and cherries or raisins to the casserole and toss gently to coat well.

3. Cover with casserole lid or vented microwave-safe clear plastic wrap. Microcook on 100% power (high) for 9 to 11 minutes or till apples are tender, stirring the mixture every 3 minutes.

4. For a smooth applesauce, mash with a potato masher. Serve warm or chilled. Sprinkle with nuts before serving. Makes about 3 cups.

CREAM-CHEESE STRUDEL

Our version of a flaky pastry found in bakeries all over Minnesota's Iron Country.

1½ cups all-purpose flour
½ cup lukewarm water
2 tablespoons cooking oil
1 slightly beaten egg yolk
½ teaspoon salt
5 tablespoons butter or margarine, melted
1 8-ounce package cream cheese, softened
¾ cup sifted powdered sugar
1 egg yolk
½ teaspoon finely shredded lemon peel or orange peel
½ teaspoon vanilla
1 egg white
1 tablespoon water

1. Mix flour, ½ cup water, oil, 1 yolk and salt. Turn onto floured surface; knead for 5 minutes. Cover with plastic wrap; let stand 1 hour.

2. Cover large surface (at least 4x3 feet) with a cloth; sprinkle with *flour*. On cloth, roll dough into 20x10-inch rectangle. Cover; let rest for 30 minutes. Brush with *2 tablespoons* of the melted butter. For filling, beat together cream cheese and powdered sugar. Beat in 1 yolk, peel and vanilla. Set aside.

3. To stretch dough, use palms of your hands and work underneath dough. Starting from middle and working toward edges, gently stretch from one corner to the next. Continue stretching till dough is paper thin, forming a 40x20-inch rectangle. Trim thick or uneven edges with scissors. Brush with remaining 3 tablespoons melted butter. Beginning 4 inches from the short side of dough, spoon filling in a 4-inch-wide band, width-wise across dough.

4. Using cloth underneath dough as a guide, gently lift the 4-inch piece of dough and lay it over filling. Slowly and evenly lift cloth and roll up dough and filling, jelly-roll style, into a tight roll. Cut off excess dough from ends to within 1 inch of filling. Fold ends under. Carefully transfer to a greased 15x10x1-inch baking pan. Curve into a C shape, making sure strudel is at least 1 inch from edge of pan.

5. Mix egg white and 1 tablespoon water. Brush over strudel. Bake in a 300° oven for 25 minutes or till golden. Carefully remove to rack; cool. Sprinkle with powdered sugar, if you like. Makes 12 servings.

KRINGLER

This rich treat from The Swedish Country Inn in Lindsborg, Kansas, is two pastries in one—a buttery piecrust-type on the bottom and a cream-puff pastry on top.

½ cup butter
1 cup all-purpose flour
1 tablespoon water
½ cup butter
1 cup all-purpose flour
3 eggs
½ teaspoon almond extract
1 cup sifted powdered
     sugar
1 tablespoon butter
   Few drops almond
     extract
   Light cream or milk

1. In a medium bowl, cut the first ½ cup butter into the first 1 cup flour till pieces are the size of small peas. Sprinkle *1 teaspoon* of the water over part of the mixture; gently toss with a fork. Push to side of bowl. Repeat till all is moistened. Shape into a ball.

2. Divide dough in half. On an ungreased baking sheet, pat or roll each piece of dough into a 12x4-inch strip. Set dough aside.

3. In a medium saucepan, combine the remaining ½ cup butter and *1 cup water*. Bring to boiling. Remove from heat; add the remaining 1 cup flour all at once. Stir the mixture vigorously till smooth. Cool for 5 minutes. Add the eggs, one at a time, beating well by hand after each addition. Stir in the ½ teaspoon almond extract.

4. Spread half of dough evenly over each pastry strip. Bake in a 375° oven for 40 minutes or till golden and puffy. Cool on wire racks.

5. Combine powdered sugar, the 1 tablespoon butter, the few drops of almond extract and enough light cream or milk to make a drizzling consistency, about 1 tablespoon. Drizzle over kringler. Cut into 1-inch diagonal slices. Makes two pastries, about 16 servings.

JAARSMA'S DUTCH LETTERS

The best we've tasted, these Dutch Letters from Jaarsma's Bakery in Pella, Iowa, require substantial preparation. We think you'll agree they're worth it.

4½ cups all-purpose flour
1 teaspoon salt
1 pound butter
1 egg
1 cup water
1 8-ounce can almond
    paste
½ cup sugar
½ cup packed brown sugar
2 egg whites
   Milk

1. Combine flour and salt. Cut butter into ½-inch slices. Stir into flour mixture, coating each butter piece to separate it (butter will be in large chunks). Combine egg and water. Add all at once to flour mixture. Mix quickly. (Butter will still be in ½-inch pieces, and flour will not be completely moistened.)

2. Turn dough onto lightly floured surface and knead 10 times, pressing and pushing dough pieces together to form a rough-looking ball. Shape dough into rectangle. (Dough still will have some dry-looking areas.) Flatten dough slightly. Working on a well-floured surface, roll out dough to a 15x10-inch rectangle. Fold 2 short sides to meet in center, then fold in half to form 4 layers (this gives a 5x7½-inch rectangle). Repeat rolling and folding process once. Cover dough with plastic wrap; chill 20 minutes. Repeat rolling and folding two more times; chill 20 minutes more.

3. For filling, combine remaining ingredients *except* milk; beat till smooth; set aside. Cut dough crosswise into 4 equal parts. Keep unused dough chilled. Roll one part of dough into a 12½x10-inch rectangle. Cut into five 10x2½-inch strips. Spread 1 slightly rounded tablespoon of filling down center of each strip; roll up lengthwise. Brush edges and ends with milk. Pinch to seal. Place seam side down on ungreased baking sheet; shape each into letter "S." Brush with milk; sprinkle with *sugar*. Repeat with remaining dough and filling. Bake in a 375° oven for 25 to 30 minutes or till golden. Cool on wire racks. Makes 20.

PUMPKIN CRÈME BRÛLÉE

Julie McVey won first place in the pudding category at the New Albany, Indiana, Harvest Baking Contest with this elegant dessert. It's a baked pumpkin custard topped with sweet caramelized sugar.

2 cups whipping cream or half-and-half
1½ tablespoons dark rum
5 egg yolks
1 cup canned pumpkin
⅓ cup sugar
1 teaspoon cornstarch
¼ teaspoon ground cinnamon
¼ teaspoon ground ginger
¼ teaspoon ground mace
⅛ teaspoon salt
½ cup sugar

1. For custard, in a heavy medium saucepan, bring the whipping cream or half-and-half and rum to boiling. Remove from heat.

2. In a bowl, beat together the egg yolks, pumpkin, ⅓ cup sugar, cornstarch, spices and salt. Gradually beat in hot cream mixture.

3. Divide custard among six 6-ounce ramekins or custard cups. Place baking dishes in a large baking pan. Pour in enough *hot water* to come halfway up the sides of the baking dishes.

4. Bake in a 350° oven for about 40 minutes or till custard is set. Remove from water and cool completely. Cover with clear plastic wrap and chill overnight. (Can be prepared as long as 2 days in advance, if you like.)

5. For topping, place ½ cup sugar in a heavy medium-size skillet over medium-high heat till sugar begins to melt, shaking skillet occasionally to heat sugar evenly. *Do not stir.* Reduce heat to low; cook till sugar is melted and golden (about 5 minutes more). Stir as necessary after the sugar begins to melt.

6. Working quickly, pour enough of the caramel mixture over each custard to almost cover the top. Tilt the dishes so the caramel mixture will cover the custard completely.

7. Refrigerate for up to 12 hours before serving. Makes 6 servings.

ENGLISH TRIFLE

Minnesotan Mona Abel, named after the British Isle of Mona, makes this family recipe using fresh summer fruits.

1 Sponge Cake or
a purchased sponge
cake or pound cake
1 6-serving-size package
instant vanilla
pudding mix
2½ cups milk
1 cup half-and-half or light
cream
⅔ cup cream sherry
1 quart fresh whole
raspberries or
strawberries, sliced
½ cup sliced almonds
½ cup whipping cream
1 tablespoon sifted
powdered sugar
1 tablespoon cream sherry

1. Cut Sponge Cake or purchased cake into 1-inch cubes (about 6 cups).

2. Prepare pudding according to package directions, using the milk and half-and-half for the liquid. (You'll use ½ cup more liquid than the box of pudding calls for.)

3. Arrange ⅓ of the cake cubes in the bottom of a 3-quart serving bowl. Drizzle ⅓ of the ⅔ cup sherry over the cake. Top with ⅓ of the berries. Then, spread with ⅓ of the pudding and sprinkle with ⅓ of the almonds. Make two more complete layers, using the same proportion of cake, sherry, berries, pudding and almonds. Cover; refrigerate for 3 to 24 hours.

4. In a mixing bowl, whip together cream, powdered sugar and 1 tablespoon sherry till stiff peaks form. Dollop on trifle. Garnish with additional berries, if you like. Serves 12.

SPONGE CAKE: Combine 1 cup *all-purpose flour* and 1 teaspoon *baking powder*. In a mixing bowl, beat 2 *eggs* with electric mixer for 4 minutes or till lemon colored. Gradually add 1 cup *sugar,* beating on medium speed for 4 to 5 minutes or till fluffy. Add flour mixture; beat at low speed just till combined.

In a saucepan, heat and stir ½ cup *milk* and 2 tablespoons *butter* or *margarine* till butter melts. Add to batter, beating till combined. Pour into a greased 9x9x2-inch baking pan. Bake in a 350° oven for 20 to 25 minutes or till done. Cool in pan on wire rack.

DECO'S RASPBERRY CHEESECAKE

At the Minnesota Museum of Art in St. Paul, The Deco Restaurant serves this light, raspberry version of a dessert favorite.

1 cup graham cracker crumbs
3 tablespoons sugar
¼ cup melted butter or margarine
1 10-ounce package frozen red raspberries, thawed
¼ cup cold water
1 envelope unflavored gelatin
1 8-ounce package cream cheese, softened
½ cup sugar
1 tablespoon Grand Marnier
1 cup whipping cream, whipped
Fresh raspberries (optional)

1. For crust, in a small bowl, combine crumbs, 3 tablespoons sugar and melted butter. Press onto the bottom of a 9-inch springform pan. Bake in a 350° oven for 10 minutes. Cool.

2. For filling, drain raspberries, reserving juice. Set raspberries aside. In a small saucepan, combine reserved juice, cold water and gelatin. Let stand for 5 minutes. Cook and stir over low heat till gelatin dissolves. Remove from heat. Cool for 10 minutes.

3. In large mixing bowl, beat cream cheese and ½ cup sugar with electric mixer on medium speed till blended. Add reserved raspberries, Grand Marnier and raspberry-gelatin mixture. Beat on low speed till well blended.

4. Chill till partially set (mixture will be consistency of unbeaten egg whites). By hand, gently fold whipped cream into partially set berry mixture. Spoon into springform pan.

5. Chill for 6 to 24 hours. Run knife around edge of pan to loosen. Remove side of pan. Top with fresh raspberries and additional whipped cream, if you like. Makes 10 servings.

STRAWBERRY-TOPPED LEMON CHEESECAKE

The Newton Band Boosters combine their homemade strawberry sauce with purchased cheesecake to sell at Troy, Ohio's Strawberry Festival. You can make your own luscious lemon-flavored cheesecake with this recipe. It's about as delicious as a cheesecake can get.

1½ cups crushed vanilla wafers
⅓ cup butter or margarine, melted
3 8-ounce packages cream cheese, softened
½ teaspoon finely shredded lemon peel
½ teaspoon vanilla
1 cup sugar
2 tablespoons all-purpose flour
2 eggs
1 egg yolk
¼ cup milk
Strawberry Sauce

1. For the crust, in a medium mixing bowl, combine the crushed vanilla wafers and melted butter. Pat crust mixture onto bottom and 1½ inches up sides of 9-inch springform pan. Place springform pan in a shallow baking pan.

2 For filling, in a large mixing bowl, beat together the cream cheese, lemon peel and vanilla with an electric mixer till fluffy. Gradually beat in the sugar and flour.

3. Add eggs and egg yolk all at once, beating on low speed till just combined. Stir in milk. Turn into prepared springform pan. Bake in a 375° oven for 35 to 40 minutes or till center appears set. Cool for 15 minutes on rack.

4. Loosen sides of cheesecake from pan with a narrow spatula. Cool for 30 minutes more. Remove sides of pan. Cool for about 2 hours more. Chill thoroughly. Serve wedges topped with the Strawberry Sauce. Store leftovers in the refrigerator. Makes 12 servings.

STRAWBERRY SAUCE: In a medium saucepan, combine 1 cup hulled crushed *strawberries,* ¾ cup *sugar,* ¼ cup *water* and 1 tablespoon *cornstarch.* (Stir in a few additional sliced berries, if you like.) Cook and stir till the mixture is thickened and bubbly. Cook and stir for 2 minutes more. Stir in 1 teaspoon *butter* or *margarine* and some *red food coloring,* if you like. Cover surface with clear plastic wrap. Chill till serving time.

WHITE CHOCOLATE CHEESECAKE

A hint of crème de cacao enhances this wonderful cheesecake from the Old Rittenhouse Inn in Bayfield, Wisconsin.

1	3-ounce package zwieback, finely crushed
2	tablespoons sugar
1	tablespoon unsweetened cocoa powder
¼	cup butter, melted
2	8-ounce packages cream cheese, softened
1	3-ounce package cream cheese, softened
5	ounces white chocolate, melted and cooled
1	cup sugar
4	teaspoons all-purpose flour
1	teaspoon vanilla
2	eggs
1	egg yolk
2	tablespoons white crème de cacao
	Chocolate Topping
	Whipped cream
	Grated chocolate

1. Combine zwieback crumbs, the 2 tablespoons sugar, cocoa and butter. Mix well. Generously butter sides of a 9-inch springform pan. Dust sides of pan with 1 tablespoon of the crumb mixture. Pat remaining crumb mixture into bottom of pan. Chill.

2. In mixing bowl, beat cream cheese, cooled white chocolate, the 1 cup sugar, flour and vanilla with an electric mixer till smooth. Add eggs and egg yolk, beating at low speed till just combined. Do not overbeat. Stir in crème de cacao. Turn into prepared crust. Bake in a 350° oven 50 to 60 minutes or till done. Cool cheesecake on rack.

3. Spread with Chocolate Topping. Chill.

4. Just before serving, garnish each serving of the cheesecake with whipped cream and grated chocolate. Makes 10 to 12 servings.

CHOCOLATE TOPPING: In saucepan, melt 2 ounces *semisweet chocolate.* Remove from heat and stir in till smooth 2 tablespoons *dairy sour cream* and 2 teaspoons *crème de cacao.* Spread on cake.

SHAPIRO'S CHOCOLATE CHEESECAKE

You won't ever be satisfied with another slice of plain cheesecake after you try this one from Shapiro's, one of the Midwest's best delis, in Indianapolis.

2 cups finely crushed graham crackers

¼ cup sugar

¼ cup butter or margarine, melted

4 8-ounce packages cream cheese, softened

1½ cups sugar

6 eggs

½ cup unsweetened cocoa powder

½ cup hot water

4 ounces unsweetened chocolate, melted and cooled (4 squares)

¼ cup butter or margarine, melted

1 tablespoon vanilla
Whipped cream
Chocolate curls
(optional)

1. In a medium mixing bowl, stir together the crushed graham crackers and ¼ cup sugar. Stir in ¼ cup melted butter or margarine. Press the mixture into the bottom and 2 inches up the sides of a 10-inch springform pan. Set aside.

2. In a large mixing bowl, beat together the softened cream cheese and 1½ cups sugar till combined. Add the eggs, one at a time, beating till combined.

3. Stir together cocoa powder and hot water. Add to cream cheese mixture.

4. Add cooled unsweetened chocolate, ¼ cup melted butter or margarine and vanilla, beating till combined.

5. Pour mixture into prepared pan. Place in a shallow baking pan in oven. Bake in a 325° oven for about 1 hour or till center appears nearly set when you shake it. Cool for 15 minutes. Loosen crust from sides of pan. Cool for 30 minutes more; remove sides of pan. Cool.

6. Cover and chill at least 4 hours. Top with whipped cream and chocolate curls, if you like. Makes 10 to 12 servings.

LINZER TORTE

The classic dessert—sort of a big, fancy almond "cookie" filled with raspberry preserves—is named for its Austrian hometown. This version comes from Ohio chef Erwin Pfeil.

1¾   cups ground almonds
1½   cups all-purpose flour
 ¾   cup sugar
 1   teaspoon finely shredded
     lemon peel
 ¼   teaspoon ground
     cinnamon
 ¼   teaspoon ground cloves
 ⅔   cup butter or margarine
 1   egg
 1   egg yolk
 1   tablespoon Kirschwasser
     (Kirsch)
 1   10-ounce jar raspberry
     preserves
 ⅓   cup sifted powdered
     sugar
 1   to 2 teaspoons
     Kirschwasser (Kirsch)

1. In a medium mixing bowl, combine almonds, flour, sugar, lemon peel, cinnamon and cloves. Cut in butter with a fork till mixture resembles coarse crumbs. Make a well in the center. Beat together egg, egg yolk and the 1 tablespoon Kirschwasser. Using a fork, stir just till dough forms a ball. Turn onto floured surface; knead 3 to 4 times.

2. With floured fingers, gently press ¾ of the dough onto bottom and 1 inch up sides of a lightly greased 10-inch springform pan. Chill remaining dough for about 20 minutes. Spread the raspberry preserves evenly over the dough in the springform pan.

3. Roll the remaining dough into a 10x6-inch rectangle. Cut six 1-inch strips. Place strips on top of preserves to resemble a lattice crust. Press ends of strips into rim of crust. Trim excess dough.

4. Bake in a 325° oven for 45 to 55 minutes or till crust is golden. Cool.

5. Meanwhile, in a small mixing bowl, combine powdered sugar and the 1 to 2 teaspoons Kirschwasser to form a glaze. Drizzle evenly over top of lattice. Cut into slices to serve. Makes 8 to 10 servings.

PASSOVER FORGOTTEN TORTE

Sharon Winstein of St. Louis says you can make both the billowy white torte and its raspberry sauce ahead of time. That's convenient for serving during the seder.

¾ cup egg whites (about 6)
    at room temperature
2 teaspoons lemon juice
¾ teaspoon vanilla
¼ teaspoon almond extract
1¼ cups sugar
1 cup whipping cream
2 teaspoons sugar
1 teaspoon vanilla
3 cups red raspberries or
    one 12-ounce package
    frozen red raspberries,
    thawed
1 tablespoon sugar
    Fresh mint leaves
    (optional)

1. Preheat oven to 450°. Grease the bottom of a 10-inch tube pan or a 9-inch springform pan. Set aside. For torte, beat egg whites, lemon juice, ¾ teaspoon vanilla and almond extract with an electric mixer on medium speed. Beat about 3 to 4 minutes or till soft peaks form (tips curl). Gradually beat in the 1¼ cups sugar, 1 tablespoon at a time, beating on high speed till stiff peaks form (tips stand straight) and sugar is almost dissolved (about 10 minutes).

2. Transfer mixture to prepared pan and smooth the top. Scrape around sides and center post (if using a tube pan), leaving a small trench between the meringue and the pan.

3. Place in preheated oven. Turn off oven. Let torte dry in oven with door closed for at least 8 hours. If using a tube pan, loosen edges and center with a sharp knife. Lift out tube. (Or remove sides of springform pan.) Slide knife under meringue. Invert onto a serving plate. Cover with plastic wrap and foil.

4. About 4 to 8 hours before serving, in a small mixing bowl, beat cream till soft peaks form. Add the 2 teaspoons sugar and 1 teaspoon vanilla; beat till stiff peaks form. Frost torte. Cover and chill till serving time.

5. For raspberry sauce, in a food processor bowl or blender container, combine berries and 1 tablespoon sugar. Cover; process or blend till smooth. Strain, if desired. Serve sauce over sliced torte. Garnish with mint, if you like. Makes 1 torte, 12 servings.

GRANDMA'S APPLE TORTE

"Even though Great Grandma is no longer with us," writes Helen Paprocki of West Allis, Wisconsin, "she's one of the crowd when we serve her special dessert. It's a festive apple pie, crowned with meringue in a crumb crust."

2 cups graham cracker crumbs
½ cup butter or margarine, melted
1 tablespoon sugar
1 cup butter or margarine
1 cup sugar
6 cups peeled and sliced cooking apples (Golden Delicious or Jonathan)
6 egg yolks
½ teaspoon ground cinnamon
½ cup chopped walnuts
4 egg whites
½ teaspoon cream of tartar
½ cup sugar

1. Combine the graham cracker crumbs, ½ cup butter or margarine and 1 tablespoon sugar. Reserve *½ cup* of the crumb mixture. Press the remaining crumb mixture into bottom and 2 inches up the sides of a 9-inch springform pan. Set the crust aside.

2. In a large saucepan, combine 1 cup butter or margarine and 1 cup sugar. Place over medium heat till butter is melted. Stir in apples. Bring to boiling. Reduce heat. Cover and cook for 10 to 12 minutes or till apples are tender, stirring occasionally.

3. In medium mixing bowl, combine egg yolks and cinnamon. Gradually stir about *1 cup* of the apple mixture into yolks. Return all the yolk mixture to the saucepan. Cook and stir over low heat for 2 minutes. Transfer to the springform pan. Sprinkle with the reserved crumbs and the nuts.

4. Bake, uncovered, in a 325° oven for 30 to 35 minutes or till center is set.

5. Meanwhile, in a large mixing bowl, beat egg whites and cream of tartar till soft peaks form (tips curl). Gradually add ½ cup sugar, beating till stiff peaks form (tips stand straight). Spread over hot apple mixture, sealing to edge.

6. Bake in a 350° oven or 15 minutes. Cool in pan for 1 hour. Chill till serving time.

7. Remove sides of springform pan. Serve warm or chilled. Store in the refrigerator. Makes 8 to 10 servings.

FUDGE POUND-CAKE SUNDAE

Patrons love this easy dessert at Ella's, everyone's favorite deli in Madison, Wisconsin.

Butter
1 ¾-inch-thick slice homemade or purchased
pound cake
3 to 4 tablespoons pur-
chased hot-fudge sauce
3 scoops French vanilla
custard ice cream
Whipped cream
Chopped nuts

1. On a lightly buttered griddle or skillet, cook cake over medium heat for 1½ to 2 minutes per side till light brown, turning once.

2. Meanwhile, heat the fudge sauce in a microwave oven or on rangetop.

3. To serve, place pound cake on dessert plate. Top with hot-fudge sauce, then the ice cream, whipped cream and nuts. Makes 1 serving.

ANGIE'S PUMPKIN ROLL

At Lucretia's restaurant in historic Ste. Genevieve, Missouri, diners choose from a dessert tray of sweets, including this seasonal pumpkin pastry.

1 cup sugar
¾ cup packaged biscuit mix
1 teaspoon pumpkin-pie
spice
1 teaspoon ground
cinnamon
½ teaspoon ground nutmeg
⅔ cup canned pumpkin
3 eggs
1 cup finely chopped nuts
Sifted powdered sugar
1 8-ounce package cream
cheese, softened
6 tablespoons butter or
margarine
1 teaspoon vanilla
1 cup sifted powdered
sugar

1. Combine sugar, biscuit mix and spices. Stir together pumpkin and eggs. Add pumpkin mixture to sugar mixture and stir till combined. Grease a 15x10x1-inch baking pan and line with waxed paper. Grease the waxed paper. Spread batter evenly into pan. Sprinkle with nuts. Bake in a 375° oven for 13 to 15 minutes or till toothpick inserted near center comes out clean. Immediately loosen edges of cake from pan and turn cake out onto a towel dusted with powdered sugar. Roll up towel and cake, jelly-roll style, starting from one of the short sides. Let cake cool on a rack.

2. To prepare filling, beat cream cheese, butter and vanilla till fluffy. Gradually add 1 cup powdered sugar, beating well. Unroll cake and remove the towel. Spread cake with filling to within 1 inch of the cake edges.

3. Roll up cake from the short side. Cover and store in the refrigerator. Serves 8 to 10.

SABAYON SAUCE

Here's just one of the outstanding desserts owner/chef David Beier prepares at his northern Michigan establishment, the Walloon Lake Inn.

4   egg yolks
⅓   cup sugar
3   tablespoons Grand
      Marnier or orange-
      flavored liqueur
1   cup whipping cream
      Fresh strawberries, hulled
      and sliced or other
      fresh fruit

1. In saucepan, beat together yolks, sugar and Grand Marnier. Cook and stir over medium-low heat for about 12 minutes or till mixture thickens to the consistency of thin cake batter. Remove from heat; chill at least 2 hours.

2. Beat cream till stiff peaks form (tips stand straight). Fold chilled egg mixture into whipping cream. Serve over fruit. Makes 2⅓ cups.

FLØTEGROT

"Cream makes it special," explains one parishioner of Our Savior's Lutheran Church near Beldenville, Wisconsin, where this pudding is served at the annual lutefisk supper.

2⅔   cups milk
3   tablespoons long-grain
      rice
2   cups whipping cream
⅔   cup all-purpose flour
3   cups milk, scalded
½   teaspoon salt
3   tablespoons sugar
½   cup sugar
1½   teaspoons ground
      cinnamon

1. Heat *2 cups* of the milk and rice to boiling. Reduce heat; cover and simmer 40 minutes or till milk is absorbed. Meanwhile, in a heavy 3-quart saucepan, bring cream and remaining ⅔ cup milk to boiling. Reduce heat to medium. Boil, gently, stirring occasionally, for 5 to 10 minutes or till mixture stops foaming.

2. Gradually sift flour into boiling cream, stirring constantly till mixture pulls away from side of the pan and butterfat separates from flour mixture. Reduce heat. Continue to cook and stir while spooning butterfat into small bowl as it accumulates. Reserve butterfat. Cook and stir till no more butterfat appears. With a wire whisk, gradually whisk in the scalded milk, stirring till smooth, velvety and mixture just comes to boiling. Add salt. Stir in rice mixture and the 3 tablespoons sugar.

3. Mix ½ cup sugar and cinnamon; serve with pudding. Pass the bowl of "butter" to spoon over pudding. Makes 8 to 10 servings.

PLUM PUDDING

Synonymous with an English Victorian Christmas, this pudding recipe comes from a holiday brunch held at the Swinney Homestead in Fort Wayne, Indiana. The pudding probably hasn't had plums in it since the 1700s. But suet is essential (ask your butcher to grind it). You can make the pudding months in advance and freeze it.

3   cups unbleached flour
2   teaspoons ground
       cinnamon
1   teaspoon baking soda
½   teaspoon salt
½   teaspoon ground cloves
½   teaspoon ground allspice
2   cups raisins
5   ounces finely ground or
       chopped beef kidney
       suet (1½ cups)
1   cup finely chopped,
       peeled apple
       (1 medium apple)
1   cup currants
1   cup light molasses
1   cup water
     Hard Sauce

1. Grease a 10-cup mold or bowl; set aside. Stir together first 6 ingredients; set aside. Combine raisins, suet, apple, currants, molasses and water; mix well. Add dry ingredients; mix thoroughly. Turn into prepared mold. Cover tightly with foil.

2. Place the filled mold on a rack in a deep kettle. Add enough *boiling water* to the kettle to cover 1 inch of the mold bottom. Cover kettle; boil gently (bubbles break surface) and steam for 3 hours. Add more boiling water, if necessary. Cool 10 minutes before unmolding onto a large piece of heavy foil. Cool 1 hour. Wrap in moisture- and vapor-proof wrap. Cool, label and freeze for up to 3 months.

3. Before serving, thaw pudding at room temperature for 3 to 4 hours. Remove foil; return the pudding to the mold. Cover the pudding and steam as above for 1 hour.

4. Slice pudding into wedges (it will be a bit crumbly). Serve with Hard Sauce. Serves 16.

HARD SAUCE: Beat ½ cup softened *butter* till fluffy. Gradually beat in 2 cups sifted *powdered sugar*. Beat in 1 teaspoon *rum extract*, ½ teaspoon *ground nutmeg* and dash *salt*. Spread in a 7½x3½x2-inch loaf pan. Cover and chill till hardened. To serve, bring to room temperature; spoon over pudding. Or, cut into squares or other shapes and serve with pudding. Makes 1¼ cups.

MENUS

EASTER BRUNCH

Champagne Fruit Bowl

Monterey Jack Cheese and Egg Casserole

Apricot-Glazed Canadian Bacon

MENUS

HEARTLAND EASTER BRUNCH

HOLIDAY TURKEY DINNER

WEEKNIGHT PASTIE DINNER

SOUP-SUPPER BUFFET

FAMILY FISH FRY

SUMMER PATIO COOKOUT

HEARTY HOMESTYLE DINNER

ITALIAN FEAST

KIDS'-CHOICE SUPPER

EASY AND ELEGANT DINNER

NO-FUSS SOUP LUNCH

PACK-A-PICNIC LUNCH

HEARTLAND EASTER BRUNCH

*Delight family and friends with this scrumptious brunch for Easter
or any other special occasion. To keep brunch-day work to a
minimum, bake the bread, assemble the egg casserole and cut up the
fruit for the fruit bowl the day before.*

Apricot-Glazed Canadian Bacon (page 26)

Monterey Jack Cheese and Egg Casserole (page 38)

Cinnamon Bread (page 82)

Hominy Grits Bake (page 68)

Champagne Fruit Bowl (page 142)

HOLIDAY TURKEY DINNER

*Although roast turkey is quite traditional, either of these stuffings will add a
unique flavor twist to that special holiday meal. Choose between the spicy dried
fruit-and-raisin stuffing or the savory vegetable-and-nut stuffing. If you like moist
stuffing, cook it in the bird. If you like drier stuffing, bake it in a casserole.*

Roast turkey

Apple-Apricot Stuffing (page 35)
or
Loggers' Vegetable Stuffing (page 34)

Spuds à la Elegant (page 72)

Buttered peas

Fresh fruit

Cheesecake-Mincemeat Pie (page 104)

WEEKNIGHT PASTIE DINNER

Take advantage of these shortcut recipes to make a workday meal a breeze. Fix the salad, vegetables and fudge sauce ahead and chill. Then just before serving assemble and bake the pasties, set out the salad and vegetables, reheat the sauce and you're ready to eat.

Quick-and-Easy Pasties (page 11)

Melba Mold Swirl (page 66)

Carrot, celery and zucchini sticks

Vanilla ice cream

Hot-Fudge Sauce (page 143)

SOUP-SUPPER BUFFET

In this menu, hot and hearty soups are just right for casual entertaining. To keep the meal simple, just add a crusty homemade bread and crisp pickles.

Hearty Buffet Chili (page 48)

Timber Charlie's Cheesy Potato Soup (page 56)

Kansas Honey-Wheat Sunflower Bread (page 77)

Assorted pickles

FAMILY FISH FRY

Fried fish and creamed corn are longtime Midwest favorites, but these new versions feature exciting flavor twists. Crispy pecans and a touch of Dijon mustard season the fish; a cream sauce brings out the sweet flavor of fresh or frozen corn.

Buttermilk-Pecan Catfish (page 37)

Creamed-Style Corn (page 70)

Tossed spinach and tomato salad with bottled Italian salad dressing

Italian bread

Zingy Zucchini Bars (page 116)

SUMMER PATIO COOKOUT

Outdoor entertaining is part of the fun of summer. Relax with friends while the meat cooks in the smoker or bakes in the oven. Then, serve buffet-style, letting your guests make their own sandwiches and come back for seconds.

Ranch-Style Brisket (page 13)

Onion buns

Old-Fashioned Sweet-Sour Coleslaw (page 64)

Fresh fruit

Dolce al Caffee (page 145)

HEARTY HOMESTYLE DINNER

*Simplify dinner-preparation chores by baking several foods in your oven
at the same time. If you're tight on oven space, use your microwave
to cook the vegetable casserole. You can make the dessert sauce ahead.
Then, quickly reheat it in the microwave oven.*

Dutch Spiced Beef (page 9)

Cheesy Broccoli Bake (page 70)

Sourdough wheat rolls

Tossed lettuce, grapefruit and orange salad with bottled oil
and vinegar salad dressing

The Sluice's Bread Pudding with Caramel Sauce (page 138)

ITALIAN FEAST

*If you're looking for a way to make friends feel special, invite them to this
delectable dinner. The meal has an Italian flavor that's sure to appeal to everyone.*

Arrorsto Vitello Maile (Veal and Pork Roast) (page 22)

Savory Baby Carrots (page 69)

Pasta with Porchini Mushroom Sauce (page 74)

Hard rolls

Fresh pears with sliced cheese

KIDS'-CHOICE SUPPER

The kids in your household will think these foods are such fun that they'll beg for them time and time again. And there's a bonus: When your youngsters want to invite their friends for supper, you'll be prepared with enough pizza and cookies to serve ten.

Puffed-Up Pizza Casserole (page 15)

Fresh vegetable dippers with purchased sour cream-onion dip

Banana and apple slices

Hunka Chocolate Cookies (page 123)

EASY AND ELEGANT DINNER

The delicious dishes will speak for themselves in this special menu. But if you'd like to dress up the meal even more, just add these extra touches. Garnish the dinner plates with orange twists, accompany the braided bread with molded butter or butter balls and accent each dessert with a few chocolate curls.

Chicken with Horseradish Cream (page 28)

Buttered asparagus spears

Molasses Whole-Wheat Braid (page 78)

Mixed salad greens, avocado and orange salad with bottled herb
and spice dressing

Raspberry Freeze (page 142)

NO-FUSS SOUP LUNCH

Don't be fooled into thinking no-fuss means no-flavor. This easy menu features a variety of seasonings that will please even the most sophisticated palate. Savor the hint of garlic and thyme in the rich tomato soup, the hearty flavors of rye flour and caraway in the yeast buns and the touch of wine that accents the ripe strawberries in the dessert.

Eagle Harbor Inn's Herbed Tomato Soup (page 41)

Sliced turkey and Swiss cheese

Quick Rye-Batter Buns (page 80)

Strawberry Nests (page 132)

PACK-A-PICNIC LUNCH

Enjoy an old-fashioned picnic in your favorite park or at the beach. Fry the chicken ahead, then chill it until serving time. Round out the meal with a couple of salads and a luscious chocolate cake. Be sure to tote all the chilled foods in a cooler with ice packs.

Fried chicken

Sweet-Potato Salad (page 60)

Missouri Botanical Gardens' Three-Bean Salad (page 63)

Husker Cola Cake (page 98)

177

Vierling Saloon's Cream of
   Chicken Soup with Wild
   Rice, 54
Vierling Saloon's Spinach-Lentil
   Soup, 56

W

Waffles, Heavenly Belgian, 87
Walnut-Cream Frosting, 95
Wheat Cinnamon Rolls, 81
Whipped Cream Topping, 102
White-Chocolate
   Cheesecake, 155
White Surprise Chili, 53
Whole-Wheat Braid,
   Molasses, 78
Whole-Wheat Bread, Luck o' the
   Irish, 79
Wiesbader Brot, 121
Wild Rice, Vierling Saloon's
   Cream of Chicken Soup
   with, 54
Wine Custard, 147
Wisconsin Potato Patties, 73

Y

Yeast Roll Dough, 20

Z

Zingerman's Noodle Kugel, 145
Zingy Zucchini Bars, 116

INDEX BY STATE